A Spiritual
Republic

Kevin T. Adam

ISBN-13: 978-1506194998
ISBN-10: 1506194990

SECOND EDITION
July, 2015

Table of Contents

Part Eight

Acknowledgements

Good books rarely come from one person's effort, and this book is no exception. Many people over the years have expressed some of the ideas presented in this book. I thank them for their contribution and applaud them for their bold thinking.

My wife Linda – This book would never have been written without her support. I'm extremely grateful for all your hard work that made this important work possible. Thank you from the bottom of my heart, and I love you. You are truly an Earth angel.

Laura Kraemer – Thank you for your time, effort, excellent proofreading, and editing. Laura's contribution helped this book to flow better and corrected "just a few" little punctuation errors and a "few" other little things too.

Sean Brennan – Thank you for the input that made the book more complete and more accessible to readers, and thank you for your time and ideas. This book is better thanks to your help.

Thanks to all the people who have, over the years, been my spiritual teachers. There have been many since I've learned something from almost everyone I've ever met. All those perspectives have led to this work; a work that I hope will help to lead America in the right direction. A work that will help our nation find its true spiritual roots so it can lead the world into our next phase of growth – working to become a peaceful and unified world.

Introduction

This country still has enormous potential, even though it's clear that politicians have wrested the United States government far from its roots as a Republic. Right now, in 2015, the U.S. government operates as a fledgling collectivist government set in place by a string of Statists. While this may seem to provide help to a modest number of citizens, that help has come at an enormous cost to the majority. So why has it changed?

The short answers are greed, and power being consolidated by a tiny percentage of wealthy and powerful citizens. Where does this leave the "average" citizen? Footing the bill for many things he did not agree to and that are not in his best interests.

In this book I'll show you that things don't have to stay this way. It's possible to run this country with integrity and within its means. I'll provide a basic road map that can help free this country from the shackles created by power-hungry politicians and CEO's. I'll show you how this country can return to being a Republic, and transform into an even greater type of government: that of a *spiritual* Republic.

Many of the ideas in this book have been around a while, and many other people have similar ideas too. That's because they're good ideas that are good for our country and good for our citizens, and the time is right to bring these ideas forward and act on them.

Even though you may have heard some of these ideas before, this book incorporates what has been, to this point, a missing element. It's the element that makes all these ideas possible. It's the element that will transform our country from the unstable society we're becoming into a secure and powerful country that can last in perpetuity. That missing element is *true spirituality*. By true spirituality I do NOT mean religion. Instead, I mean embracing the root spiritual tenets that are the foundation of *all* spiritually-based religions. The principles I'll be covering apply to all true religions and exclude none. These principles, applied as a foundation to form the new basis of our country, will yield a strong, stable, and respectful society of spiritually aware citizens.

Some readers will think this is a pie-in-the-sky dream that will never materialize. It won't if that is our starting point and belief. Instead, let's start with the premise that it *can* happen. Let's approach this from the perspective of thinking about what we can do to *make* it happen. We *can* do this, and we can start now. I say this because I know this country can be much more than it is now, and even greater than we have been in the past. Although "American exceptionalism" is currently not much more than American egotism, we can regain that exceptionalism and grow even further by more and more Americans learning about the true nature of spirituality and our place in this universe.

My motivation in bringing out the information in this book is simple. I know this country can do better and be more than it is. I want to help move us away from the brink of destruction we're approaching. I think all Americans deserve that. I think the *world* deserves that too since America as a spiritual Republic will serve as a shining example for others to emulate, and will help to lead this world into global peace and prosperity.

I can't directly prove many of the spiritual principles I'll be writing about. Even though I can't directly prove these principles, many of them will resound in your heart as right and true. Follow that feeling because it will lead you to greater spiritual awareness. At the very least give these ideas some thought and consideration. See if you can at least agree that these ideas are positive steps. If you honestly consider the ideas I'll be presenting, you'll most likely come to understand that people will benefit from us collectively taking a more spiritual and harmonious perspective.

I recognize that, at this point, most readers will have no real reason to believe anything I say. Right now, I ask only for the chance to earn some of your trust. As you read, look at the root ideas I'm expressing and see if these ideas resonate in your heart. See if there is consistency in my message, for consistency is often found in the truth. I honestly appreciate your trust and you taking the time to consider the messages I'm trying to convey. A strong, prosperous America and, eventually, a world at peace will come as we deepen our spiritual foundation. *Our best chance at achieving these two lofty goals comes from discovering our true spiritual nature.*

10

We can each do our part to bring this about by studying our true spiritual nature and by helping others around us to do the same. That is the root that makes the rest possible. If you want America to be a strong, prosperous nation that will provide safety and security for our children, grandchildren, and all future generations, then join me on this crusade to help our country reach the true greatness it can have. Help me transform America into a spiritual Republic.

Kevin Adam
January, 2015

Added note: In this book I'll be using two terms that many people think mean the same thing, but the way I'll be using these terms are essentially polar opposites. The two terms are *politicians* and *statesmen.* Here is the definition of each term as found on dictionary.com:

Politician: A seeker or holder of public office who is more concerned about winning favor or retaining power than about maintaining principles.

Statesman: A person who exhibits great wisdom and ability in directing the affairs of a government or in dealing with important public issues. In addition, I'm adding the supposition that the Statesman works for the people, and is not for sale to special interests.

For additional clarification, here is an explanatory excerpt also from dictionary.com: "Politician, statesman refer to one skilled in politics. These terms differ particularly in their connotations; politician is more often derogatory, and statesman laudatory. Politician suggests the schemes and devices of a person who engages in (especially small) politics for party ends or for one's own advantage: a dishonest politician. Statesman suggests the eminent ability, foresight, and unselfish patriotic devotion of a person dealing with (especially important or great) affairs of state: a distinguished statesman."

A Spiritual Republic

Part One: Where we are today

It's clear that this country has seen better days. What began as a bold experiment has, from its inception, been beset by those who would have done things differently. In the 227 years since the Constitution has been ratified, numerous influences have tried to change the course of our nation and wrest it off its foundation. Their efforts have met with some success and our country is in a tattered condition as a result. Fortunately, our best years can still be ahead of us if we begin to correct the damage that has been done to our nation. Although it will take a great deal of effort and some time, we can still successfully grow into a spiritual Republic.

Many different people in many different roles have had a hand in driving us into the difficult position we find ourselves in today. Let's take a look at some hard data that, at least to me, clearly shows what desperate straits this country is actually in. I'm confident that most reasonable people who look at this information objectively will also come to realize that the United States is quickly running out of rope. There will be those who choose to deny it, despite the facts, but denial won't change the truth. The sooner we accept the truth and begin to make the tough decisions and take the tough actions, the better chance we have of pulling back from the precipice and not leaving a crippled and destitute country to posterity.

****

I had a list of metrics that I thought would fairly well represent the conditions we're currently facing here in the U.S.. After considering this list, I narrowed it down to three that I think will clearly show we have some work to do in order to avert serious negative consequences. The three I chose are: 1) Government deficits and the national debt; 2) Civil Liberties, specifically freedom of the press and property rights; and 3) Economic and business freedom.

The first information we'll look at is a spreadsheet I assembled to compare our Gross Domestic Product from 2000 to 2013, along with our national debt, the interest on that debt, and government surpluses or deficits for each year. The spreadsheet is on the next page, and you'll see some alarming recent trends that may create a feeling of dread in the pit of your stomach if you haven't seen this information before. All of the information was gathered from government sources, and those sources are indicated on the chart.

The numbers on the chart are in billions, so all those numbers also have *six* zeroes after them. This means the GDP numbers and national debt numbers are all *trillions*. Keep in mind that this data ends in 2013, so the hole we're in is noticeably deeper now. In other words, things have gotten worse, not better. Take a look at the chart:

Year	GDP	National debt	%GDP	Interest	Net interest rate	Federal surplus/deficit
2000	$10,285	$5,674	55.17%	$362.0	6.38%	$236.2
2001	$10,622	$5,807	54.67%	$359.5	6.19%	$128.2
2002	$10,978	$6,228	56.73%	$332.5	5.34%	-$157.8
2003	$11,511	$6,783	58.93%	$318.1	4.69%	-$377.6
2004	$12,275	$7,379	60.11%	$321.6	4.36%	-$412.7
2005	$13,094	$7,932	60.58%	$352.3	4.44%	-$318.3
2006	$13,856	$8,507	61.40%	$405.9	4.77%	-$248.2
2007	$14,478	$9,007	62.21%	$430.0	4.77%	-$160.7
2008	$14,719	$10,024	68.10%	$451.1	4.50%	-$458.6
2009	$14,419	$11,910	82.60%	$383.1	3.22%	-$1,412.7
2010	$14,964	$13,561	90.62%	$413.9	3.05%	-$1,294.4
2011	$15,518	$14,790	95.31%	$454.4	3.07%	-$1,299.6
2012	$16,163	$16,066	99.40%	$359.8	2.24%	-$1,087.0
2013	$16,768	$16,738	99.82%	$415.7	2.48%	-$679.5

Notes: Source for GDP is the USDC Bureau of Economic Analysis

National debt amounts are as of fiscal y/e, which is 9/30

Interest amounts are from treasurydirect.gov

Federal surplus/deficit taken from spreadsheets downloaded from whitehouse.gov

All amounts are in billions of dollars

Anyone who looks at these numbers and doesn't think our country is in deep trouble is absolutely in denial. Things *cannot* continue this way if we want to survive as a nation. If you're not convinced, then think about it from a personal point of view. How comfortable would you feel if you owed more on your credit cards than you made in a year? Would you feel as though you had a strong, stable financial foundation for your family, or would you feel some measure of desperation? Probably the latter. And keep in mind that this isn't like having a mortgage. This isn't *secured* debt – other than the assurance of "backed by the full faith and credit of the United States." From my perspective, we're already maxed out – but Washington keeps spending.

We're going to take a look at one item more closely – Federal surpluses or deficits from 1990 to 2013. This will tell us what years we spent more money than we had, and how much we had to borrow. And just to bring this up, before we get into that data – who do we owe that money to? Here is a chart that shows the breakdown as of May 2014. The list starts with the biggest slice of the pie on top and goes in descending order.

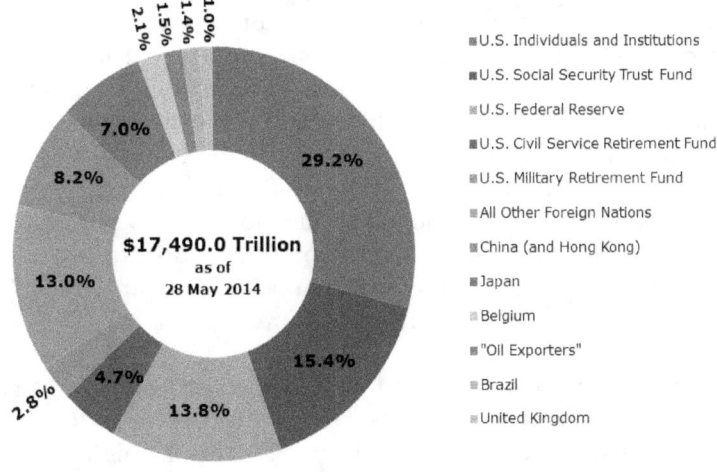

Summer 2014: To Whom Does the U.S. Government Owe Money?

$17,490.0 Trillion as of 28 May 2014

29.2% · 15.4% · 13.8% · 4.7% · 2.8% · 13.0% · 8.2% · 7.0% · 2.1% · 1.5% · 1.4% · 1.0%

- U.S. Individuals and Institutions
- U.S. Social Security Trust Fund
- U.S. Federal Reserve
- U.S. Civil Service Retirement Fund
- U.S. Military Retirement Fund
- All Other Foreign Nations
- China (and Hong Kong)
- Japan
- Belgium
- "Oil Exporters"
- Brazil
- United Kingdom

Sources: U.S. Treasury Department, U.S. Federal Reserve   © Political Calculations 2014

As you can see, the largest holders are U.S. individuals and institutions, with Social Security next. As of December 1, 2014, our national debt topped $18 trillion dollars, which means the Social Security portion at that time was about $2.7 trillion dollars. Perhaps that has something to do with Social Security running out of money....

Let's look at Federal government deficits from 1990 to 2013. It shows what I would consider an alarming trend. Here is a chart with that data:

Fed Govt Annual Deficits and Surpluses 1990-2013
(In Billions)

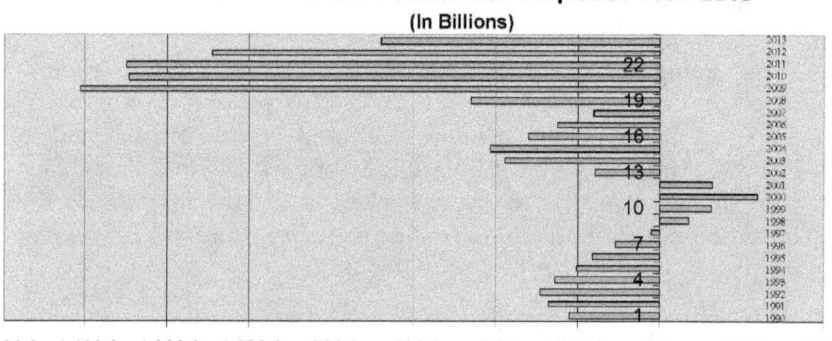

I'm no Nobel Laureate economist, but it seems to me that spending far more than you make every year can't work for very long. I believe that should be fairly obvious, even to our current crop of politicians. Sadly, they don't seem to understand the simple fact that this behavior has made things worse for our country and its citizens, and that politicians have bankrupted this nation. Imagine what straits your family would be in if you spent 30% more than you made every year. They'd be dire to be sure, and you'd be headed for bankruptcy as well. If you're not sure we're bankrupt, keep in mind that our national debt now exceeds our GDP and that gap will continue to widen into the future.

I know I'm not the only person who recognizes this. I know I'm not the only person who realizes we're on the edge of a cliff and we need to make immediate and drastic changes if this nation is to survive. In fact, our government *knows* this path isn't sustainable yet they have kept us on it anyway. With that in mind, do you genuinely believe the government has the best interests of all Americans in mind? I think any answer but "no" is rooted in denial and blind, unjustified faith. The next page has a screen capture from the U.S. Government Accountability Office website, and their opinion about the sustainability of our deficit spending is posted on the Web for everyone to see. You'll see that opinion toward the bottom of the image.

Of course, debt is not our only issue. Poverty and unemployment are significant indicators of our financial health, and these numbers paint a dim picture as well. The Stanford Center on Poverty and Inequality published their annual "National Report Card" in January 2014. In that Report they indicated that 15% of our total population lives in poverty.

This is from page 5 of the report in the Executive Summary:

RISING POVERTY

- The official poverty rate increased from 12.5 percent in 2007 to 15.0 percent in 2012, and the child poverty rate increased from 18.0 percent in 2007 to 21.8 percent in 2012. The current poverty rates for the full population and for children rank among the very worst over the 13 years since 2000 (i.e., both are ranked 11th).
- The latter increases in poverty, although substantial, would have been yet larger had the effects of the labor market downturn not been countered with aggressive safety net programs. Absent any safety net benefits in 2012, the supplemental poverty measure would have been 14.5 points higher.

The same report addresses unemployment. In a table on page 8, the official unemployment rate at the time the report was prepared was 7.8%. But what does this mean? How does the government define "unemployment"? That question doesn't have a simple answer, and it seems that the government definition has evolved over time when things needed to look more favorable. The current definition of unemployment is being willing and able to work, have worked in the past year, and have "actively" sought employment some time over the last 4 *weeks*. That's a narrow window, and it's likely that this window has shrunk over time to improve the statistics. I

Key Issues > Fiscal Outlook > Federal Fiscal Outlook

Fiscal Outlook: Federal Fiscal Outlook

GAO's federal budget simulations provide a broad context for considering policy options. An understanding of fiscal exposures —programs that may expose the government to future spending—can also inform these considerations.

View the Spring 2014 Update

OVERVIEW | CURRENT OUTLOOK | ASSUMPTIONS & DATA | FISCAL EXPOSURES | KEY REPORTS | GAO CONTACT

Since 1992, GAO has published long-term fiscal simulations showing federal deficits and debt under different sets of policy assumptions. While the timing and pace of growth varies depending on the assumptions used, GAO's simulations illustrate that:

- A fundamental imbalance between revenue and spending over the long term leads to continuous growth in debt as a share of gross domestic product (GDP), which is unsustainable.
- Increases in spending are driven by an aging population and rising health care costs.
- The growing gap between revenue and spending will further limit the federal government's flexibility to address future challenges.

Federal Budget Path is Unsustainable over the Long Term

GAO runs two simulations. In the Baseline Extended simulation, which generally assumes current law continues, debt as a share of gross domestic product (GDP) declines in the short term before turning up again. In the Alternative simulation, in which some assumptions are changed to reflect historical trends, federal debt as a share of GDP grows throughout the period. These simulations show that, without policy changes, debt held by the public will surpass its historical high within the next 15-20 years searched for but couldn't find older definitions, so unfortunately I can't prove my assertion. Perhaps I'm wrong and that's been the official definition for many years. However, the official rate doesn't tell the whole story.

There is a category of workers identified as *discouraged*. These folks have worked within the past year, are able and willing to work, but haven't "actively" sought employment within the last 4 weeks according to the government's definition. This category, as listed in the National Report Card at the time it was published, shows an unemployment rate of *8.3 percent* and this percentage isn't included in the official definition – so they're dropped off. To me, this seems like bureaucratic legerdemain. They're still unemployed, willing and able to work, but haven't met the government's criteria to be listed as "actively" seeking employment. If we add discouraged workers to the "official" percentage, the employment rate at the time of this publication was *16.1 percent*. It is likely lower now, but keep this information in mind: The actual unemployment rate is probably closer to *double* what the government indicates.

Too many Americans seem to be OK with resting on our laurels and not looking at the data objectively. As a result, many Americans still believe we are the wealthiest and "best" nation on the planet. But are we, and how rich are we really? As a country, we owe more than we make every year and have 15% of our population living in poverty. Does that seem like a rich country? Can we honestly say we, as a country, are rich? The truth hurts sometimes, and the answer is an obvious and emphatic "no."

Civil liberties

Our civil liberties have been chipped at and broken away over the past five or so decades. We really aren't a truly free nation at this point in our history. There are several independent analysis groups that score and rate the nations of the world to see how they compare with each other. One of these groups is the Economist Intelligence Unit, or EIU. It's a sister company of The Economist newspaper, and here is an excerpt from the "About" page of their website:

"We are the research and analysis division of The Economist Group, the sister company to *The Economist* newspaper.

Created in 1946, we have nearly 70 years' experience in helping businesses, financial firms and governments to understand how the world is changing and how that creates opportunities to be seized and risks to be managed. A British company, we are intensely global."

One of their reports is the Democracy Index, and the 2013 version of this report shows a table on page three showing the overall democracy rank of each nation, with the most democratic topping the list. Here is a segment of the list that shows the top 19 nations:

Table 2
Democracy Index 2013

	Overall score	Rank	Electoral process	Functioning of government	Political participation
			Full democracies		
Norway	9.93	1	10.00	9.64	10.00
Sweden	9.73	2	9.58	9.64	9.44
Iceland	9.65	3	10.00	9.64	8.89
Denmark	9.38	4	9.58	9.64	8.89
New Zealand	9.26	5	10.00	9.29	8.89
Australia	9.13	6	9.58	8.93	7.78
Switzerland	9.09	7	9.58	9.29	7.78
Canada	9.08	8	9.58	9.29	7.78
Finland	9.03	9	10.00	8.93	7.78
Luxembourg	8.88	10	10.00	9.29	6.67
Netherlands	8.84	11	9.58	8.21	8.89
Ireland	8.68	12	9.58	7.86	7.22
Austria	8.48	13	9.58	7.50	7.78
United Kingdom	8.31	14	9.58	7.14	6.67
Germany	8.31	15	9.58	7.50	7.22
Malta	8.28	16	9.17	8.21	5.56
Uruguay	8.17	=17	10.00	8.93	4.44
Mauritius	8.17	=17	9.17	8.21	5.00
USA	8.11	19	9.17	7.50	7.22

Look down the list. You'll see the United States at the bottom of this segment in *19th* place. In checking the 2014 version of this report, I discovered there was no change in U.S. ranking. I would bet that most Americans would think our country would be at or near the top of the list, and we probably have been in the past. I think 19th place is much too far down the list for the "land of the free and the home of the brave." We can and *should* do better – much better. You can find the full report and more information about how they generate their rankings on their website www.eiu.com.

Freedom of the press

Now let's consider freedom of the press. This is another category in which I believe most Americans would rate our nation highly. They'd unfortunately be disappointed. We'll look at the *Freedom of the Press Report* from Freedom House. Here is how they describe their organization on their website, www.freedomhouse.org:

"Freedom House is an independent watchdog organization dedicated to the expansion of freedom around the world.

Today, as more than two billion people live under oppressive rule, Freedom House speaks out against the main threats to democracy and empowers citizens to exercise their fundamental rights. We analyze the challenges to freedom; advocate for greater political and civil liberties; and support frontline activists to defend human rights and promote democratic change. Founded in 1941, Freedom House was the first American organization to champion the advancement of freedom globally."

We'll look at the data from their 2014 report, and here is a description of the scoring in the report from their website:

"The *Freedom of the Press* report measures the level of media independence in 197 countries and territories. Each country receives a numerical score from 0 (the most free) to 100 (the least free) on the basis of combined scores from three subcategories: the legal environment (A), the political environment (B), and the economic environment (C). For each category, a lower number of points is allotted for a more free situation, while a higher number of points is allotted for a less free environment."

The next graphic, found on page 6 of the report, shows the change in selected country's scores, comparing 2012 to 2013:

BIGGEST GAINS AND DECLINES 2012–2013

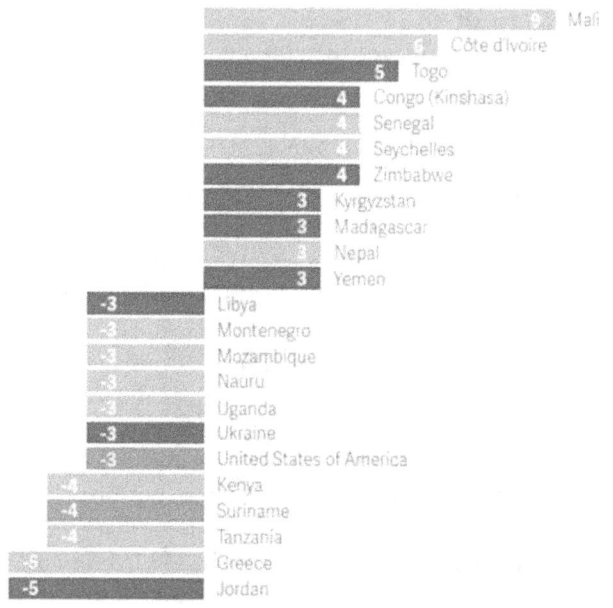

This chart clearly shows that the United States has lost three points of measurement in just one year. Now let's look at the top of another chart in the report, found on page 20:

FREEDOM
OF THE PRESS
2014

Press Freedom in 2013: Media Freedom Hits Decade Low

GLOBAL RANKINGS

Rank 2014	Country	Score	Status
1	Netherlands	10	Free
	Norway	10	Free
	Sweden	10	Free
4	Belgium	11	Free
	Finland	11	Free
6	Denmark	12	Free
	Iceland	12	Free
	Luxembourg	12	Free

Let's look deeper into that chart to see if we can find U.S. ranking:

26	Canada	19	Free
27	Bahamas	20	Free
	Czech Republic	20	Free
	St. Kitts and Nevis	20	Free
30	Austria	21	Free
	Micronesia	21	Free
	United States of America	21	Free
33	Australia	22	Free
	Belize	22	Free
	France	22	Free
36	Malta	23	Free
	Slovakia	23	Free
	United Kingdom	23	Free
39	Grenada	24	Free
	Lithuania	24	Free
	Slovenia	24	Free

20

... and there we are, in **32nd** place.

The *Freedom of the Press 2014* report has information in it about how they arrived at their rankings. You can get the report from www.freedomhouse.org.

Property rights
We'll use data from the Heritage Foundation to look at several metrics: overall world rank, property rights rank, and the U.S. rank

for freedom from corruption. Some of the following information came from their report, the *2014 Index of Economic Freedom*. I also downloaded the spreadsheet from their website, www.heritage.org, and sorted it to find the following rankings for the U.S.:

Overall economic freedom: 12th place
Property rights: 24th place
Freedom from corruption: 24th place

Not something to be proud of, to be sure. And, for a bit more bad news, overall we've been getting *worse*. Here is a graphic from page two of the *2014 Index of Economic Freedom*, showing that America has declined in economic freedom for seven years in a row:

AMERICA IN DECLINE

By sharp contrast, the **United States** has been on the opposite path as the only country to have recorded a loss of economic freedom for seven straight years.

Ease of doing business and economic freedom

We mentioned overall economic freedom in the previous section, and now we'll look at some numbers that rate economic freedom in the context of how easy it is to do business in the United States. This information comes from the *Doing Business 2014* report, produced by World Bank and available on the website www.doingbusiness.org.

This next chart is from page three of *Doing Business 2014*, and shows the overall world rankings in ease of doing business. We did better here, ranking in fourth place:

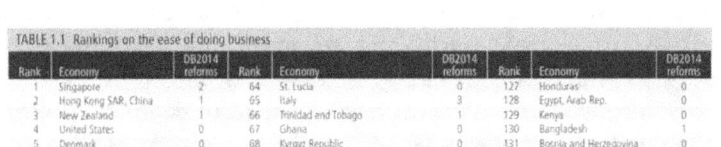

This next chart is from page four of the Heritage Foundation's *2014 Index of Economic Freedom Report* showing the United States in 12th place:

RANKING THE WORLD BY ECONOMIC FREEDOM

Rank	Country	Overall Score	Rank	Country	Overall Score	Rank	Country	C
1	Hong Kong	90.1	66	Ghana	64.2	132	Papua New Guinea	
2	Singapore	89.4	67	Kazakhstan	63.7	133	Guinea	
3	Australia	82.0	68	Montenegro	63.6	134	Mauritania	
4	Switzerland	81.6	69	Portugal	63.5	135	Egypt	
5	New Zealand	81.2	70	France	63.5	136	Cameroon	
6	Canada	80.2	71	Panama	63.4	137	China	
7	Chile	78.7	72	Thailand	63.3	138	Liberia	
8	Mauritius	76.5	73	Trinidad and Tobago	62.7	139	Tajikistan	
9	Ireland	76.2	74	Slovenia	62.7	140	Russia	
10	Denmark	76.1	75	South Africa	62.5	141	Burundi	
11	Estonia	75.9	76	Kuwait	62.3	142	Comoros	
12	United States	75.5	77	Saudi Arabia	62.2	143	Guinea-Bissau	
13	Bahrain	75.1	78	Paraguay	62.0	144	Laos	
14	United Kingdom	74.9	79	Madagascar	61.7	145	Maldives	

What can we do about this?

In a short answer, we have to make the changes necessary to turn this country around. Part of the problem is the Fed artificially forcing interest rates to at or near zero. The most likely outcome of raising interest rates is a recession, and that recession could be a factor for a long time – perhaps a decade or more.

The main reason raising rates could trigger a recession is that American consumption is fueled by borrowing instead of cash as in the past. As rates increase, people will be able to "afford" fewer things and will be forced to buy less. This weakened consumption will decrease demand, leading to a decrease in production. This could lead to a downward spiral in employment and possibly trigger a depression.

We can solve this problem by making it easier for businesses to grow. If we focus on actions that generate business profits, we'll be boosting the economy through more and better paying jobs. This in turn will allow a gradual increase in interest rates without triggering a recession. Increased business revenues also leads to larger government revenue through increased tax payments. No tax rate increase will be needed to generate these extra revenues. Instead, we can create additional revenue and strengthen our economy by removing choking regulations that only use up resources and do nothing for our environment or economy – other than bloating bureaucracy and creating a bigger government.

More government jobs may look, on the surface, as something that will benefit the economy by employing more people, but that is not at all true. Those jobs are not *productive* jobs that produce revenue. They're *expense* jobs that rob revenue. Decreasing the size of the government and the number of government jobs will serve to increase our productivity and prosperity.

It's true that decreasing the size of the government will decrease the number of government jobs available. These jobs, however, are not lost. Decreasing the size of the government decreases government operating expenses – and all those expenses are, in one way or another, paid for by business revenue. This decrease in government size, if appropriately accompanied by a decrease in unnecessary government regulations, makes businesses more profitable.

More profit means growth and more jobs. The primary difference between most of these private jobs and the government jobs they'll replace is that a percentage of the private jobs will be productive. This increase in production will add to our GDP. As a bonus, increasing production leads to increased profits, and more business profit leads to more jobs and more tax revenue for the government.

Another one of our problems is that too many people in our society have gotten too accustomed to government bailouts. Whether it's families on social assistance who could be working but aren't, or irresponsible, overpaid business executives who expect the government (ie, *taxpayers*) to pay for their risk taking and failed financial manipulations, or anyone in between, too many Americans look to the government for an easy handout. What they fail (or refuse) to recognize is that it's their fellow Americans – the citizens who work hard and pay taxes – that are really footing the bill. This goes strongly against the spiritual principle of self-responsibility.

Rest assured that I'm not saying families who genuinely need help shouldn't get it. Far from that. All of us want people who need the help to have it. But some program reforms are needed to get able-bodied people back to work to restore their self-respect as they generate their own income which, of course, generates more income taxes and increases self-esteem.

I could go on and on, deeper into the mess we're in right now, but there are many – and probably hundreds – of books that go into detail about how we got into this mess and who is responsible for what parts of it. In reality, none of that is important. What is important is clearly recognizing where we are and then creating plans to solve these massive problems.

The problem is real. Politicians have created this problem over a long period of time and we let them do it. The only way to fix this problem is to change the kind of politician we send to Washington. We need to elect statesmen who want to work for the American people and who want to do what's right – and who won't be corrupted by power. That may seem difficult right now, but it's a necessary step and something we can accomplish. Some of the newer politicians are leaning this way and we can, over time, change the way Washington operates. I believe that we, as citizens of this nation, have the power and responsibility to restore ethical leadership to our country. I'll get further into how we can do that in Chapter Six.

A Spiritual Republic

Part Two: What the Founders and Framers intended

I strongly believe the Founders and Framers incorporated some spiritual principles into parts of our founding documents, although most of the statements in the Declaration and Constitution deal with purely practical matters. I've include the text of both documents in this section, including the Amendments.

If you've never read these documents before, or if it's been a long time since you have, I ask that you at least read through them before reading further in this book. You'll see paragraphs where I interject between segments and explain what spiritual principles I believe apply. We'll start at the beginning – with the Declaration of Independence.

The Declaration of Independence
IN CONGRESS, July 4, 1776

The unanimous Declaration of the thirteen united States of America,

When in the Course of human events, it becomes necessary for one people to dissolve the political bands which have connected them with another, and to assume among the powers of the earth, the separate and equal station to which the Laws of Nature and of Nature's God entitle them, a decent respect to the opinions of mankind requires that they should declare the causes which impel them to the separation.

We hold these truths to be self-evident, that all men are created equal, that they are endowed by their Creator with certain unalienable Rights, that among these are Life, Liberty and the pursuit of Happiness. — That to secure these rights, Governments are instituted among Men, deriving their just powers from the consent of the governed, — That whenever any Form of Government becomes destructive of these ends, it is the Right of the People to alter or to abolish it, and to institute new Government, laying its foundation on such principles and organizing its powers in such form, as to them shall seem most likely to effect their Safety and Happiness.

Prudence, indeed, will dictate that Governments long established should not be changed for light and transient causes; and accordingly all experience hath shewn, that mankind are more disposed to suffer, while evils are sufferable, than to right themselves by abolishing the forms to which they are accustomed. But when a long train of abuses and usurpations, pursuing invariably the same Object evinces a design to reduce them under absolute Despotism, it is their right, it is their duty, to throw off such Government, and to provide new Guards for their future security. — Such has been the patient sufferance of these Colonies; and such is now the necessity which constrains them to alter their former Systems of Government. The history of the present King of Great Britain is a history of repeated injuries and usurpations, all having in direct object the establishment of an absolute Tyranny over these States. To prove this, let Facts be submitted to a candid world.

(There are clear spiritual references in these two opening paragraphs. They recognize God and Natural Law, and that each person is equal under God's Law. They reference liberty as God-given and a man who seeks to end liberty as a tyrant. The spiritual principle of self-responsibility comes into play as the Founders indicate they are compelled to take action to end the tyranny. Underlying the concepts in both these paragraphs is the Universal Law of Free Will.)

He has refused his Assent to Laws, the most wholesome and necessary for the public good.

He has forbidden his Governors to pass Laws of immediate and pressing importance, unless suspended in their operation till his Assent should be obtained; and when so suspended, he has utterly neglected to attend to them.

He has refused to pass other Laws for the accommodation of large districts of people, unless those people would relinquish the right of Representation in the Legislature, a right inestimable to them and formidable to tyrants only.

(In these three segments the Founders recognized the importance of maintaining civil laws as a means to ensure the natural right of liberty. They also recognize the extreme value of that right and that taking away natural rights is a means to controlling and subjugating citizens.)

He has called together legislative bodies at places unusual, uncomfortable, and distant from the depository of their public Records, for the sole purpose of fatiguing them into compliance with his measures.

He has dissolved Representative Houses repeatedly, for opposing with manly firmness his invasions on the rights of the people.

He has refused for a long time, after such dissolutions, to cause others to be elected; whereby the Legislative powers, incapable of Annihilation, have returned to the People at large for their exercise; the State remaining in the mean time exposed to all the dangers of invasion from without, and convulsions within.

He has endeavoured to prevent the population of these States; for that purpose obstructing the Laws for Naturalization of Foreigners; refusing to pass others to encourage their migrations hither, and raising the conditions of new Appropriations of Lands.

He has obstructed the Administration of Justice, by refusing his Assent to Laws for establishing Judiciary powers.

He has made Judges dependent on his Will alone, for the tenure of their offices, and the amount and payment of their salaries.

He has erected a multitude of New Offices, and sent hither swarms of Officers to harrass our people, and eat out their substance.

He has kept among us, in times of peace, Standing Armies without the Consent of our legislatures.

He has affected to render the Military independent of and superior to the Civil power.

He has combined with others to subject us to a jurisdiction foreign to our constitution, and unacknowledged by our laws; giving his Assent to their Acts of pretended Legislation:
For Quartering large bodies of armed troops among us:

For protecting them, by a mock Trial, from punishment for any Murders which they should commit on the Inhabitants of these States:

(All of these preceding segments depict a King who has usurped the citizen's natural rights, which are given by God and not granted by the King. This assuredly violates the spiritual Laws of Free Will, Self-Responsibility, and Harmlessness.)

For cutting off our Trade with all parts of the world:

For imposing Taxes on us without our Consent:

For depriving us in many cases, of the benefits of Trial by Jury:

For transporting us beyond Seas to be tried for pretended offences:

For abolishing the free System of English Laws in a neighbouring Province, establishing therein an Arbitrary government, and enlarging its Boundaries so as to render it at once an example and fit instrument for introducing the same absolute rule into these Colonies:

For taking away our Charters, abolishing our most valuable Laws, and altering fundamentally the Forms of our Governments:

For suspending our own Legislatures, and declaring themselves invested with power to legislate for us in all cases whatsoever.

He has abdicated Government here, by declaring us out of his Protection and waging War against us.

(The preceding four segments all identify a tyrant who has stolen the colonist's natural liberty and clearly violated the Universal Law of Free Will.)

He has plundered our seas, ravaged our Coasts, burnt our towns, and destroyed the lives of our people.

He is at this time transporting large Armies of foreign Mercenaries to compleat the works of death, desolation and tyranny, already begun with circumstances of Cruelty &

perfidy scarcely paralleled in the most barbarous ages, and totally unworthy the Head of a civilized nation.

He has constrained our fellow Citizens taken Captive on the high Seas to bear Arms against their Country, to become the executioners of their friends and Brethren, or to fall themselves by their Hands.

He has excited domestic insurrections amongst us, and has endeavoured to bring on the inhabitants of our frontiers, the merciless Indian Savages, whose known rule of warfare, is an undistinguished destruction of all ages, sexes and conditions.

In every stage of these Oppressions We have Petitioned for Redress in the most humble terms: Our repeated Petitions have been answered only by repeated injury. A Prince whose character is thus marked by every act which may define a Tyrant, is unfit to be the ruler of a free people.

(The last sentence is quite important. It demonstrates that the colonists are very aware they are indeed a free people and possess natural and God-given rights. They properly identify tyranny and their right to overthrow that tyranny.)

Nor have We been wanting in attentions to our British brethren. We have warned them from time to time of attempts by their legislature to extend an unwarrantable jurisdiction over us. We have reminded them of the circumstances of our emigration and settlement here. We have appealed to their native justice and magnanimity, and we have conjured them by the ties of our common kindred to disavow these usurpations, which, would inevitably interrupt our connections and correspondence. They too have been deaf to the voice of justice and of consanguinity. We must, therefore, acquiesce in the necessity, which denounces our Separation, and hold them, as we hold the rest of mankind, Enemies in War, in Peace Friends.

We, therefore, the Representatives of the united States of America, in General Congress, Assembled, appealing to the Supreme Judge of the world for the rectitude of our intentions, do, in the Name, and by Authority of the good People of these Colonies, solemnly publish and declare, That these United Colonies are, and of Right ought to be Free and Independent States; that they are Absolved from all

Allegiance to the British Crown, and that all political connection between them and the State of Great Britain, is and ought to be totally dissolved; and that as Free and Independent States, they have full Power to levy War, conclude Peace, contract Alliances, establish Commerce, and to do all other Acts and Things which Independent States may of right do. And for the support of this Declaration, with a firm reliance on the protection of divine Providence, we mutually pledge to each other our Lives, our Fortunes and our sacred Honor.

(The reference to "the Supreme Judge of the world" in the first sentence is clearly a reference to God and not a man. In the last section the Colonists demonstrate that they are following a right and just course of action in making this declaration and believe they thus have God on their side.)

The Constitution of the United States
September 17, 1787

We the People of the United States, in Order to form a more perfect Union, establish Justice, insure domestic Tranquility, provide for the common defence, promote the general Welfare, and secure the Blessings of Liberty to ourselves and our Posterity, do ordain and establish this Constitution for the United States of America.

(This opening segment, the Preamble, clearly establish the new nation as one firmly based on preserving liberty for the citizens of the time and for all United States citizens into the unending future.)

Article. I.

Section. 1. All legislative Powers herein granted shall be vested in a Congress of the United States, which shall consist of a Senate and House of Representatives.

Section. 2. The House of Representatives shall be composed of Members chosen every second Year by the People of the several States, and the Electors in each State shall have the Qualifications requisite for Electors of the most numerous Branch of the State Legislature.

No Person shall be a Representative who shall not have attained to the Age of twenty five Years, and been seven Years a Citizen of the United States, and who shall not, when elected, be an Inhabitant of that State in which he shall be chosen.

Representatives and direct Taxes shall be apportioned among the several States which may be included within this Union,
according to their respective Numbers, which shall be determined by adding to the whole Number of free Persons, including those bound to Service for a Term of Years, and excluding Indians not taxed, three fifths of all other Persons. The actual Enumeration shall be made within three Years after the first Meeting of the Congress of the United States, and within every subsequent Term of ten Years, in such Manner as they shall by Law direct. The Number of Representatives shall not exceed one for every thirty Thousand, but each State shall have at Least one Representative; and until such enumeration shall be made, the State of New Hampshire shall be entitled to chuse three, Massachusetts eight, Rhode-Island and Providence Plantations one, Connecticut five, New-York six, New Jersey four, Pennsylvania eight, Delaware one, Maryland six, Virginia ten, North Carolina five, South Carolina five, and Georgia three.

(The reference "three fifths of all other Persons" was intended to account in some way for slaves. We know slavery was a hotly contested topic and concessions for slavery appear throughout the Constitution. What I don't understand is why some proponents of slavery were able to uphold that slaves were property even though the Constitution refers to them as "Persons," although partial persons. Perhaps not all Supreme Court Justices truly intended to uphold the Constitution and wanted to reform or even eliminate it right away. That process seems to have continued throughout our history and into today.)

When vacancies happen in the Representation from any State, the Executive Authority thereof shall issue Writs of Election to fill such Vacancies.

The House of Representatives shall chuse their Speaker and other Officers; and shall have the sole Power of Impeachment.

Section. 3. The Senate of the United States shall be composed of two Senators from each State, chosen by the

Legislature thereof, for six Years; and each Senator shall have one Vote.

Immediately after they shall be assembled in Consequence of the first Election, they shall be divided as equally as may be into three Classes.

The Seats of the Senators of the first Class shall be vacated at the Expiration of the second Year, of the second Class at the

Expiration of the fourth Year, and of the third Class at the Expiration of the sixth Year, so that one third may be chosen every second Year; and if Vacancies happen by Resignation, or otherwise, during the Recess of the Legislature of any State, the Executive thereof may make temporary Appointments until the next Meeting of the Legislature, which shall then fill such Vacancies.

No Person shall be a Senator who shall not have attained to the Age of thirty Years, and been nine Years a Citizen of the United States, and who shall not, when elected, be an Inhabitant of that State for which he shall be chosen.

The Vice President of the United States shall be President of the Senate, but shall have no Vote, unless they be equally divided.

The Senate shall chuse their other Officers, and also a President pro tempore, in the Absence of the Vice President, or when he shall exercise the Office of President of the United States.

The Senate shall have the sole Power to try all Impeachments. When sitting for that Purpose, they shall be on Oath or Affirmation.

When the President of the United States is tried, the Chief Justice shall preside: And no Person shall be convicted without the Concurrence of two thirds of the Members present.

Judgment in Cases of Impeachment shall not extend further than to removal from Office, and disqualification to hold and enjoy any Office of honor, Trust or Profit under the United States: but the Party convicted shall nevertheless be liable and subject to Indictment, Trial, Judgment and Punishment, according to Law.

Section. 4. The Times, Places and Manner of holding Elections for Senators and Representatives, shall be prescribed in each State by the Legislature thereof; but the Congress may at any time by Law make or alter such Regulations, except as to the Places of chusing Senators.

The Congress shall assemble at least once in every Year, and such Meeting shall be on the first Monday in December, unless they shall by Law appoint a different Day.

Section. 5. Each House shall be the Judge of the Elections, Returns and Qualifications of its own Members, and a Majority of each shall constitute a Quorum to do Business; but a smaller Number may adjourn from day to day, and may be authorized to compel the Attendance of absent Members, in such Manner, and under such Penalties as each House may provide.

Each House may determine the Rules of its Proceedings, punish its Members for disorderly Behaviour, and, with the Concurrence of two thirds, expel a Member.

Each House shall keep a Journal of its Proceedings, and from time to time publish the same, excepting such Parts as may in their Judgment require Secrecy; and the Yeas and Nays of the Members of either House on any question shall, at the Desire of one fifth of those Present, be entered on the Journal.

Neither House, during the Session of Congress, shall, without the Consent of the other, adjourn for more than three days, nor to any other Place than that in which the two Houses shall be sitting.

Section. 6. The Senators and Representatives shall receive a Compensation for their Services, to be ascertained by Law, and paid out of the Treasury of the United States. They shall in all Cases, except Treason, Felony and Breach of the Peace, be privileged from Arrest during their Attendance at the Session of their respective Houses, and in going to and returning from the same; and for any Speech or Debate in either House, they shall not be questioned in any other Place.

No Senator or Representative shall, during the Time for which he was elected, be appointed to any civil Office under the Authority of the United States, which shall have been created, or the Emoluments whereof shall have been encreased during such time; and no Person holding any Office under the United States, shall be a Member of either House during his Continuance in Office.

Section. 7. All Bills for raising Revenue shall originate in the House of Representatives; but the Senate may propose or concur with Amendments as on other Bills.

Every Bill which shall have passed the House of Representatives and the Senate, shall, before it become a Law, be presented to the President of the United States; If he approve he shall sign it, but if not he shall return it, with his Objections to that House in which it shall have originated, who shall enter the Objections at large on their Journal, and proceed to reconsider it. If after such Reconsideration two thirds of that House shall agree to pass the Bill, it shall be sent, together with the Objections, to the other House, by which it shall likewise be reconsidered, and if approved by two thirds of that House, it shall become a Law. But in all such Cases the Votes of both Houses shall be determined by yeas and Nays, and the Names of the Persons voting for and against the Bill shall be entered on the Journal of each House respectively. If any Bill shall not be returned by the President within ten Days (Sundays excepted) after it shall have been presented to him, the Same shall be a Law, in like Manner as if he had signed it, unless the Congress by their Adjournment prevent its Return, in which Case it shall not be a Law.

Every Order, Resolution, or Vote to which the Concurrence of the Senate and House of Representatives may be necessary (except on a question of Adjournment) shall be presented to the President of the United States; and before the Same shall take Effect, shall be approved by him, or being disapproved by him, shall be repassed by two thirds of the Senate and House of Representatives, according to the Rules and Limitations prescribed in the Case of a Bill.

Section. 8. The Congress shall have Power To lay and collect Taxes, Duties, Imposts and Excises, to pay the Debts and provide for the common Defence and general Welfare of the United States; but all Duties, Imposts and Excises shall be uniform throughout the United States;

To borrow Money on the credit of the United States;

To regulate Commerce with foreign Nations, and among the several States, and with the Indian Tribes;

To establish an uniform Rule of Naturalization, and uniform Laws on the subject of Bankruptcies throughout the United States;

To coin Money, regulate the Value thereof, and of foreign Coin, and fix the Standard of Weights and Measures;

To provide for the Punishment of counterfeiting the Securities and current Coin of the United States;

To establish Post Offices and post Roads;

To promote the Progress of Science and useful Arts, by securing for limited Times to Authors and Inventors the exclusive Right to their respective Writings and Discoveries;

To constitute Tribunals inferior to the supreme Court;

To define and punish Piracies and Felonies committed on the high Seas, and Offenses against the Law of Nations;

To declare War, grant Letters of Marque and Reprisal, and make Rules concerning Captures on Land and Water;

To raise and support Armies, but no Appropriation of Money to that Use shall be for a longer Term than two Years;

To provide and maintain a Navy;

To make Rules for the Government and Regulation of the land and naval Forces;

To provide for calling forth the Militia to execute the Laws of the Union, suppress Insurrections and repel Invasions;

To provide for organizing, arming, and disciplining, the Militia, and for governing such Part of them as may be employed in the Service of the United States, reserving to the States respectively, the Appointment of the Officers, and the Authority of training the Militia according to the discipline prescribed by Congress;

To exercise exclusive Legislation in all Cases whatsoever, over such District (not exceeding ten Miles square) as may, by Cession of particular States, and the Acceptance of Congress, become the Seat of the Government of the United States, and to exercise like Authority over all Places purchased by the Consent of the Legislature of the State in which the Same shall be, for the Erection of Forts, Magazines, Arsenals, dock-Yards, and other needful Buildings; — And To make all Laws which shall be necessary and proper for carrying into Execution the foregoing Powers, and all other Powers vested by this Constitution in the

Government of the United States, or in any Department or Officer thereof.

Section. 9. The Migration or Importation of such Persons as any of the States now existing shall think proper to admit, shall not be prohibited by the Congress prior to the Year one thousand eight hundred and eight, but a Tax or duty may be imposed on such Importation, not exceeding ten dollars for each Person.

The Privilege of the Writ of Habeas Corpus shall not be suspended, unless when in Cases of Rebellion or Invasion the public Safety may require it.

No Bill of Attainder or ex post facto Law shall be passed.

No Capitation, or other direct, Tax shall be laid, unless in Proportion to the Census or Enumeration herein before directed to be taken.

No Tax or Duty shall be laid on Articles exported from any State.

No Preference shall be given by any Regulation of Commerce or Revenue to the Ports of one State over those of another: nor shall Vessels bound to, or from, one State, be obliged to enter, clear, or pay Duties in another.

No Money shall be drawn from the Treasury, but in Consequence of Appropriations made by Law; and a regular Statement and Account of the Receipts and Expenditures of all public Money shall be published from time to time.

No Title of Nobility shall be granted by the United States: And no Person holding any Office of Profit or Trust under them, shall, without the Consent of the Congress, accept of any present, Emolument, Office, or Title, of any kind whatever, from any King, Prince, or foreign State.

Section. 10. No State shall enter into any Treaty, Alliance, or Confederation; grant Letters of Marque and Reprisal; coin Money; emit Bills of Credit; make any Thing but gold and silver Coin a Tender in Payment of Debts; pass any Bill of Attainder, ex post facto Law, or Law impairing the Obligation of Contracts, or grant any Title of Nobility.

No State shall, without the Consent of the Congress, lay any Imposts or Duties on Imports or Exports, except what may be absolutely necessary for executing it's inspection Laws: and the net Produce of all Duties and Imposts, laid by any State on Imports or Exports, shall be for the Use of the Treasury of the United States; and all such Laws shall be subject to the Revision and Control of the Congress.

No State shall, without the Consent of Congress, lay any Duty of Tonnage, keep Troops, or Ships of War in time of Peace, enter into any Agreement or Compact with another State, or with a foreign Power, or engage in War, unless actually invaded, or in such imminent Danger as will not admit of delay.

Article. II.

Section. 1. The executive Power shall be vested in a President of the United States of America. He shall hold his Office during the Term of four Years, and, together with the Vice President, chosen for the same Term, be elected, as follows:

Each State shall appoint, in such Manner as the Legislature thereof may direct, a Number of Electors, equal to the whole Number of Senators and Representatives to which the State may be entitled in the Congress: but no Senator or Representative, or Person holding an Office of Trust or Profit under the United States, shall be appointed an Elector.

The Electors shall meet in their respective States, and vote by Ballot for two Persons, of whom one at least shall not be an Inhabitant of the same State with themselves. And they shall make a List of all the Persons voted for, and of the Number of Votes for each; which List they shall sign and certify, and transmit sealed to the Seat of the Government of the United States, directed to the President of the Senate. The President of the Senate shall, in the Presence of the Senate and House of Representatives, open all the Certificates, and the Votes shall then be counted. The Person having the greatest Number of Votes shall be the President, if such Number be a Majority of the whole Number of Electors appointed; and if there be more than one who have such Majority, and have an equal Number of Votes, then the House of Representatives shall immediately chuse by Ballot one of them for President; and if no Person have a Majority, then from the five highest on the List the said House shall in like Manner chuse the President. But in chusing the President, the Votes shall be taken by States, the Representation from each State having one Vote; A

quorum for this purpose shall consist of a Member or Members from two thirds of the States, and a Majority of all the States shall be necessary to a Choice. In every Case, after the Choice of the President, the Person having the greatest Number of Votes of the Electors shall be the Vice President. But if there should remain two or more who have equal Votes, the Senate shall chuse from them by Ballot the Vice President.

(This process has more merit than may be obvious on the surface. The Constitution does not require political parties. Instead, the Framers allowed for the person receiving the greatest number of votes to be named President, and the person receiving the second greatest number of votes named as Vice President. While this surely presents problems in a party system, this actually does something very important for the citizens. What this provision does is increase the number of citizens whose votes are represented at the Executive level. Here's how: in a two person election [for simplicity] the winner may have won by a narrow margin, say 51% to 49%. With the system as outlined in the Constitution, the entire population is represented in the government executives – either the President or the Vice President. Therefore, a greater percentage of citizens have their wishes honored in choosing the executives. In other words, all the citizens voted for one or the other, so both take office. Without parties, and within the framework of a spiritual Republic [more specifics are in Part Four], this situation could work out very well and is something we can consider when our country is ready for this type of arrangement.)

The Congress may determine the Time of chusing the Electors, and the Day on which they shall give their Votes; which Day shall be the same throughout the United States.

No Persons except a natural born Citizen, or a Citizen of the United States, at the time of the Adoption of this Constitution, shall be eligible to the Office of President; neither shall any Person be eligible to that Office who shall not have attained to the Age of thirty five Years, and been fourteen Years a Resident within the United States.

In Case of the Removal of the President from Office, or of his Death, Resignation, or Inability to discharge the Powers and Duties of the said Office, the Same shall devolve on the Vice President, and the Congress may by Law provide for the Case of Removal, Death, Resignation or Inability, both of the President and Vice President, declaring what Officer shall then act as President, and such Officer shall act accordingly, until the Disability be removed, or a President shall be elected.

The President shall, at stated Times, receive for his Services, a Compensation, which shall neither be increased nor diminished during the Period for which he shall have been elected, and he shall not receive within that Period any other Emolument from the United States, or any of them.

Before he enter on the Execution of his Office, he shall take the following Oath or Affirmation: — "I do solemnly swear (or affirm) that I will faithfully execute the Office of President of the United States, and will to the best of my Ability, preserve, protect and defend the Constitution of the United States."

Section. 2. The President shall be Commander in Chief of the Army and Navy of the United States, and of the Militia of the
several States, when called into the actual Service of the United States; he may require the Opinion, in writing, of the principal Officer in each of the executive Departments, upon any Subject relating to the Duties of their respective Offices, and he shall have Power to grant Reprieves and Pardons for Offences against the United States, except in Cases of Impeachment.

He shall have Power, by and with the Advice and Consent of the Senate, to make Treaties, provided two thirds of the Senators present concur; and he shall nominate, and by and with the Advice and Consent of the Senate, shall appoint Ambassadors, other public Ministers and Consuls, Judges of the supreme Court, and all other Officers of the United States, whose Appointments are not herein otherwise provided for, and which shall be established by Law: but the Congress may by Law vest the Appointment of such inferior Officers, as they think proper, in the President alone, in the Courts of Law, or in the Heads of Departments.

The President shall have Power to fill up all Vacancies that may happen during the Recess of the Senate, by granting Commissions which shall expire at the End of their next Session.

Section. 3. He shall from time to time give to the Congress Information of the State of the Union, and recommend to their Consideration such Measures as he shall judge necessary and expedient; he may, on extraordinary Occasions, convene both Houses, or either of them, and in Case of Disagreement between them, with Respect to the Time of Adjournment, he may adjourn them to such Time as he shall think proper; he shall receive Ambassadors and other public Ministers; he shall take Care that the Laws be faithfully executed, and shall Commission all the Officers of the United States.

Section. 4. The President, Vice President and all civil Officers of the United States, shall be removed from Office on Impeachment for, and Conviction of, Treason, Bribery, or other high Crimes and Misdemeanors.

(The phrase "high Crimes and Misdemeanors" originated long ago in the English Parliament and essentially means an official abusing their political power for personal gain. You can find more information about this term online on a variety of websites. Although the language is dated the intent of the phrase still stands.)

Article. III.

Section. 1. The judicial Power of the United States, shall be vested in one supreme Court, and in such inferior Courts as the Congress may from time to time ordain and establish. The Judges, both of the supreme and inferior Courts, shall hold their Offices during good Behaviour, and shall, at stated Times, receive for their Services, a Compensation, which shall not be diminished during their Continuance in Office.

Section. 2. The judicial Power shall extend to all Cases, in Law and Equity, arising under this Constitution, the Laws of the United States, and Treaties made, or which shall be made, under their Authority; — to all Cases affecting Ambassadors, other public Ministers and Consuls; — to all Cases of admiralty and maritime Jurisdiction; — to Controversies to which the United States shall be a Party; — to Controversies between two or more States; — between a

State and Citizens of another State; — between Citizens of different States; — between Citizens of the same State claiming Lands under Grants of different States, and between a State, or the Citizens thereof, and foreign States, Citizens or Subjects.

In all Cases affecting Ambassadors, other public Ministers and Consuls, and those in which a State shall be Party, the supreme Court shall have original Jurisdiction. In all the other Cases before mentioned, the supreme Court shall have appellate Jurisdiction, both as to Law and Fact, with such Exceptions, and under such Regulations as the Congress shall make. The Trial of all Crimes, except in Cases of Impeachment, shall be by Jury; and such Trial shall be held in the State where the said Crimes shall have been committed; but when not committed within any State, the Trial shall be at such Place or Places as the Congress may by Law have directed.

Section. 3. Treason against the United States, shall consist only in levying War against them, or in adhering to their Enemies, giving them Aid and Comfort. No Person shall be convicted of Treason unless on the Testimony of two Witnesses to the same overt Act, or on Confession in open Court.

The Congress shall have Power to declare the Punishment of Treason, but no Attainder of Treason shall work Corruption of Blood, or Forfeiture except during the Life of the Person attained.

Article. IV.
Section. 1. Full Faith and Credit shall be given in each State to the public Acts, Records, and judicial Proceedings of every other State. And the Congress may by general Laws prescribe the Manner in which such Acts, Records and Proceedings shall be proved, and the Effect thereof.

Section. 2. The Citizens of each State shall be entitled to all Privileges and Immunities of Citizens in the several States.

A Person charged in any State with Treason, Felony, or other Crime, who shall flee from Justice, and be found in another State, shall on Demand of the executive Authority of the State from which he fled, be delivered up, to be removed to the State having Jurisdiction of the Crime.

No Person held to Service or Labour in one State, under the Laws thereof, escaping into another, shall, in Consequence of any Law or Regulation therein, be discharged from such Service or Labour, but shall be delivered up on Claim of the Party to whom such Service or Labour may be due.

Section. 3. New States may be admitted by the Congress into this Union; but no new State shall be formed or erected within the Jurisdiction of any other State; nor any State be formed by the Junction of two or more States, or Parts of States, without the Consent of the Legislatures of the States concerned as well as of the Congress.

The Congress shall have Power to dispose of and make all needful Rules and Regulations respecting the Territory or other Property belonging to the United States; and nothing in this Constitution shall be so construed as to Prejudice any Claims of the United States, or of any particular State.

Section. 4. The United States shall guarantee to every State in this Union a Republican Form of Government, and shall protect each of them against Invasion; and on Application of the Legislature, or of the Executive (when the Legislature cannot be convened) against domestic Violence.

Article. V.
The Congress, whenever two thirds of both Houses shall deem it necessary, shall propose Amendments to this Constitution, or, on the Application of the Legislatures of two thirds of the several States, shall call a Convention for proposing Amendments, which, in either Case, shall be valid to all Intents and Purposes, as Part of this Constitution, when ratified by the Legislatures of three fourths of the several States, or by Conventions in three fourths thereof, as the one or the other Mode of Ratification may be proposed by the Congress; Provided that no Amendment which may be made prior to the Year One thousand eight hundred and eight shall in any Manner affect the first and fourth Clauses in the Ninth Section of the first Article; and that no State, without its Consent, shall be deprived of its equal Suffrage in the Senate.

Article. VI.

All Debts contracted and Engagements entered into, before the Adoption of this Constitution, shall be as valid against the United States under this Constitution, as under the Confederation.

This Constitution, and the Laws of the United States which shall be made in Pursuance thereof; and all Treaties made, or which shall be made, under the Authority of the United States, shall be the supreme Law of the Land; and the Judges in every State shall be bound thereby, any Thing in the Constitution or Laws of any State to the Contrary notwithstanding.

The Senators and Representatives before mentioned, and the Members of the several State Legislatures, and all executive and judicial Officers, both of the United States and of the several States, shall be bound by Oath or Affirmation, to support this Constitution; but no religious Test shall ever be required as a Qualification to any Office or public Trust under the United States.

Article. VII.

The Ratification of the Conventions of nine States, shall be sufficient for the Establishment of this Constitution between the States so ratifying the Same.

Attest William Jackson, Secretary
done in Convention by the Unanimous Consent of the States present the Seventeenth Day of September in the Year of our Lord one thousand seven hundred and Eighty seven and of the Independence of the United States of America the Twelfth

In Witness
whereof We have hereunto subscribed our Names,
Go. Washington—
Presidt. and deputy from Virginia

Amendments to the Constitution of the United States

The first ten Amendments are the Bill of Rights and were ratified December 15. 1791.

Amendment I
Congress shall make no law respecting an establishment of religion, or prohibiting the free exercise thereof; or abridging the freedom of speech, or of the press; or the right of the people peaceably to assemble, and to petition the Government for a redress of grievances.

(The first Amendment states that the government will not establish a State or National religion. This leaves the people with the right to choose to worship as they see fit and includes the choice to not participate in any form of religion.)

Amendment II
A well regulated militia, being necessary to the security of a free State, the right of the people to keep and bear arms, shall not be infringed.

Amendment III
No soldier shall, in time of peace be quartered in any house, without the consent of the owner, nor in time of war, but in a manner to be prescribed by law.

Amendment IV
The right of the people to be secure in their persons, houses, papers, and effects, against unreasonable searches and seizures, shall not be violated, and no warrants shall issue, but upon probable cause, supported by oath or affirmation, and particularly describing the place to be searched, and the persons or things to be seized.

Amendment V
No person shall be held to answer for a capital, or otherwise infamous crime, unless on a presentment or indictment of a Grand Jury, except in cases arising in the land or naval forces, or in the militia, when in actual service in time of war or public danger; nor shall any person be subject for the same offence to be twice put in jeopardy of life or limb; nor shall be compelled in any criminal case to be a witness, against himself, nor be deprived of life, liberty, or property, without due process of law; nor shall private property be taken for public use, without just compensation.

(The fourth and fifth Amendments recognize the spiritual principle of liberty and the concept of being presumed innocent without any evidence of wrongdoing.)

Amendment VI
In all criminal prosecutions, the accused shall enjoy the right to a speedy and public trial, by an impartial jury of the State and district wherein the crime shall have been committed, which district shall have been previously ascertained by law, and to be informed of the nature and cause of the accusation; to be confronted with the witnesses against him; to have compulsory process for obtaining witnesses in his favor, and to have the assistance of counsel for his defense.

Amendment VII
In suits at common law, where the value in controversy shall exceed twenty dollars, the right of trial by jury shall be preserved, and no fact tried by a jury, shall be otherwise re-examined in any court of the United States, than according to the rules of the common law.

Amendment VIII
Excessive bail shall not be required, nor excessive fines imposed, nor cruel and unusual punishments inflicted.

Amendment IX
The enumeration in the Constitution, of certain rights, shall not be construed to deny or disparage others retained by the people.

Amendment X
The powers not delegated to the United States by the Constitution, nor prohibited by it to the States, are reserved to the States, respectively, or to the people.

Amendment XI - Ratified Feb. 7, 1795
The judicial power of the United States shall not be construed to extend to any suit in law or equity, commenced or prosecuted against one of the United States by citizens of another State, or by citizens or subjects of any foreign state.

Amendment XII - Ratified July 27, 1804
(Amended by the 20th Amendment, Sections 3 and 4)
The electors shall meet in their respective states, and vote by ballot for President and Vice President, one of whom, at least, shall not be an inhabitant of the same state with themselves; they shall name in their ballots the person voted for as President, and in distinct ballots the person voted for as Vice President, and they shall make distinct lists of all persons

voted for as President, and of all persons voted for as Vice President, and of the number of votes for each, which lists they shall sign and certify, and transmit sealed to the seat of the government of the United States, directed to the President of the Senate; the President of the Senate shall, in the presence of the Senate and House of Representatives, open all the certificates and the votes shall then be counted; the person having the greatest number of votes for President, shall be the President, if such number be a majority of the whole number of electors appointed; and if no person have such majority, then from the persons having the highest numbers not exceeding three on the list of those voted for as President, the House of Representatives shall choose immediately, by ballot, the President.

But in choosing the President, the votes shall be taken by states, the representation from each State having one vote; a quorum for this purpose shall consist of a member or members from two thirds of the states, and a majority of all the states shall be necessary to a choice. And if the House of Representatives shall not choose a President whenever the right of choice shall devolve upon them, before the fourth day of March next following, then the Vice President shall act as President, as in the case of the death or other constitutional disability of the President. The person having the greatest number of votes as Vice President, shall be the Vice President, if such number be a majority of the whole number of electors appointed, and if no person have a majority, then from the two highest numbers on the list, the Senate shall choose the Vice President; a quorum for the purpose shall consist of two thirds of the whole number of Senators, and a majority of the whole number shall be necessary to a choice. But no person constitutionally ineligible to the office of President shall be eligible to that of Vice President of the United States.

Amendment XIII – Ratified Dec. 6, 1865
Section 1
Neither slavery nor involuntary servitude, except as a punishment for crime whereof the party shall have been duly convicted, shall exist within the United States, or any place subject to their jurisdiction.

Section 2
Congress shall have power to enforce this article by appropriate legislation.

Amendment XIV – Ratified July 9, 1868
Section 1
All persons born or naturalized in the United States, and subject to the jurisdiction thereof, are citizens of the United States and of the State wherein they reside. No State shall make or enforce any law which shall abridge the privileges or immunities of citizens of the United States; nor shall any State deprive any person of life, liberty, or property, without due process of law; nor deny to any person within its jurisdiction the equal protection of the laws.

Section 2
Representatives shall be apportioned among the several States according to their respective numbers, counting the whole number of persons in each State, excluding Indians not taxed. But when the right to vote at any election for the choice of electors for President and Vice President of the United States, Representatives in Congress, the executive and judicial officers of a State, or the members of the Legislature thereof, is denied to any of the male inhabitants of such State, being twenty-one years of age, and citizens of the United States, or in any way abridged, except for participation in rebellion, or other crime, the basis of representation therein shall be reduced in the proportion which the number of such male citizens shall bear to the whole number of male citizens twenty-one years of age in such State.

Section 3
No person shall be a Senator or Representative in Congress, or elector of President and Vice President, or hold any office, civil or military, under the United States, or under any State, who, having previously taken an oath, as a member of Congress, or as an officer of the United States, or as a member of any State Legislature, or as an executive or judicial officer of any State, to support the Constitution of the United States, shall have engaged in insurrection or rebellion against the same, or given aid or comfort to the enemies thereof. But Congress may, by a vote of two thirds of each House, remove such disability.

Section 4
The validity of the public debt of the United States, authorized by law, including debts incurred for payment of pensions and bounties for services in suppressing insurrection or rebellion, shall not be questioned. But neither the United States nor any

State shall assume or pay any debt or obligation incurred in aid of insurrection or rebellion against the United States, or any claim for the loss or emancipation of any slave; but all such debts, obligations, and claims shall be held illegal and void.

Section 5
The Congress shall have power to enforce, by appropriate legislation, the provisions of this article.

Amendment XV - Ratified Feb. 3, 1870
Section 1
The right of citizens of the United States to vote shall not be denied or abridged by the United States or by any State on account of race, color, or previous condition of servitude.

Section 2
The Congress shall have power to enforce this article by appropriate legislation.

Amendment XVI – Ratified Feb. 3, 1913
The Congress shall have power to lay and collect taxes on incomes, from whatever source derived, without apportionment among the several States, and without regard to any census or enumeration.

Amendment XVII – Ratified April 8, 1913
The Senate of the United States shall be composed of two Senators from each State, elected by the people thereof, for six years; and each Senator shall have one vote. The electors in each State shall have the qualifications requisite for electors of the most numerous branch of the State Legislatures.

When vacancies happen in the representation of any State in the Senate, the executive authority of such State shall issue writs of election to fill such vacancies: Provided, that the legislature of any State may empower the executive thereof to make temporary appointment until the people fill the vacancies by election as the legislature may direct.

This amendment shall not be so construed as to affect the election or term of any Senator chosen before it becomes valid as part of the Constitution.

Amendment XVIII - Ratified by three quarters of the states by Jan. 16, 1919, and became effective Jan. 16, 1920
*Repealed by the 21st Amendment.
Section 1
After one year from the ratification of this article the manufacture, sale, or transportation of intoxicating liquors within, the importation thereof into, or the exportation thereof from the United States and all territory subject to the jurisdiction thereof for beverage purposes is hereby prohibited.

Section 2
The Congress and the several States shall have concurrent power to enforce this article by appropriate legislation.

Section 3
This article shall be inoperative unless it shall have been ratified as an amendment to the Constitution by the legislatures of the several States, as provided in the Constitution, within seven years from the date of the submission hereof to the States by Congress.

Amendment XIX – Ratified Aug. 18, 1920
The right of citizens of the United States to vote shall not be denied or abridged by the United States or by any State on account of sex.

Congress shall have power to enforce this article by appropriate legislation.

Amendment XX - Ratified Jan. 23, 1933
Section 1
The terms of the President and Vice President shall end at noon on the twentieth day of January, and the terms of Senators and Representatives at noon on the third day of January, of the years in which such terms would have ended if this article had not been ratified; and the terms of their successors shall then begin.

Section 2
The Congress shall assemble at least once in every year, and such meeting shall begin at noon on the third day of January, unless they shall by law appoint a different day.

Section 3

If, at the time fixed for the beginning of the term of the President, the President-elect shall have died, the Vice President-elect shall become President. If a President shall not have been chosen before the time fixed for the beginning of his term, or if the President-elect shall have failed to qualify, then the Vice President shall have qualified; and the Congress may by law provide for the case wherein neither a President-elect nor a Vice President-elect shall have qualified, declaring who shall then act as President, or the manner in which one who is to act shall be selected, and such person shall act accordingly until a President or Vice President shall have qualified.

Section 4

The Congress may by law provide for the case of the death of any of the persons from whom the House of Representatives may choose a President whenever the right of choice shall have devolved upon them, and for the case of the death of any of the persons from whom the Senate may choose a Vice President whenever the right of choice shall have devolved upon them.

Section 5

Sections 1 and 2 shall take effect on the 15th day of October following the ratification of this article.

Section 6

This article shall be inoperative unless it shall have been ratified as an amendment to the Constitution by the legislatures of three fourths of the several States within seven years from the date of its submission.

Amendment XXI - Ratified Dec. 5, 1933
Section 1

The eighteenth article of amendment to the Constitution of the United States is hereby repealed.

Section 2

The transportation or importation into any State, territory, or possession of the United States for delivery or use therein of intoxicating liquors, in violation of the laws thereof, is hereby prohibited.

54

Section 3

This article shall be inoperative unless it shall have been ratified as an amendment to the Constitution by convention in the several States, as provided in the Constitution, within seven years from the date of the submission thereof to the States by the Congress.

Amendment XXII – Ratified Feb. 27, 1951
Section 1

No person shall be elected to the office of the President more than twice, and no person who has held the office of President, or acted as President, for more than two years of a term to which some other person was elected President shall be elected to the office of the President more than once. But this article shall not apply to any person holding the office of President when this article was proposed by the Congress, and shall not prevent any person who may be holding the office of President, or acting as President, during the term within which this article becomes operative from holding the office of President or acting as President during the remainder of such term.

Section 2

This article shall be inoperative unless it shall have been ratified as an amendment to the Constitution by the legislatures of three fourths of the several States within seven years from the date of its submission to the States by the Congress.

Amendment XXIII – Ratified March 29, 1961
Section 1

The District constituting the seat of Government of the United States shall appoint in such manner as the Congress may direct: A number of electors of President and Vice President equal to the whole number of Senators and Representatives in Congress to which the District would be entitled if it were a State, but in no event more than the least populous State; they shall be in addition to those appointed by the States, but they shall be considered, for the purposes of the election of President and Vice President, to be electors appointed by a State; and they shall meet in the District and perform such duties as provided by the twelfth article of amendment.

Section 2
The Congress shall have the power to enforce this article by appropriate legislation.

Amendment XXIV - Ratified Jan. 23, 1964
Section 1
The right of citizens of the United States to vote in any primary or other election for President or Vice President, for electors for President or Vice President, or for Senator or Representative in Congress, shall not be denied or abridged by the United States or any State by reasons of failure to pay any poll tax or other tax.

Section 2
The Congress shall have the power to enforce this article by appropriate legislation.

Amendment XXV – Ratified Feb. 10, 1967
Section 1
In case of the removal of the President from office or of his death or resignation, the Vice President shall become President.

Section 2
Whenever there is a vacancy in the office of the Vice President, the President shall nominate a Vice President who shall take office upon confirmation by a majority vote of both Houses of Congress.

Section 3
Whenever the President transmits to the President pro tempore of the Senate and the Speaker of the House of Representatives his written declaration that he is unable to discharge the powers and duties of his office, and until he transmits to them a written declaration to the contrary, such powers and duties shall be discharged by the Vice President as Acting President.

Section 4
Whenever the Vice President and a majority of either the principal officers of the executive departments or of such other body as Congress may by law provide, transmit to the President pro tempore of the Senate and the Speaker of the House of Representatives their written declaration that the President is unable to discharge the powers and duties of his

office, the Vice President shall immediately assume the powers and duties of the office as Acting President.

Thereafter, when the President transmits to the President pro tempore of the Senate and the Speaker of the House of Representatives his written declaration that no inability exists, he shall resume the powers and duties of his office unless the Vice President and a majority of either the principal officers of the executive department or of such other body as Congress may by law provide, transmit within four days to the President pro tempore of the Senate and the Speaker of the House of Representatives their written declaration that the President is unable to discharge the powers and duties of his office. Thereupon Congress shall decide the issue, assembling within forty-eight hours for that purpose if not in session. If the Congress, within twenty-one days after receipt of the latter written declaration, or, if Congress is not in session, within twenty-one days after Congress is required to assemble, determines by two thirds vote of both Houses that the President is unable to discharge the powers and duties of his office, the Vice President shall continue to discharge the same as Acting President; otherwise, the President shall resume the powers and duties of his office.

Amendment XXVI - Ratified July 1, 1971
Section 1
The right of citizens of the United States, who are 18 years of age or older, to vote shall not be denied or abridged by the United States or by any state on account of age.

Section 2
The Congress shall have power to enforce this article by appropriate legislation.

Amendment XXVII
(The proposed amendment was sent to the states Sept. 25, 1789, by the First Congress. It was ratified May 7, 1992.)
No law, varying the compensation for the services of the Senators and Representatives, shall take effect, until an election of Representatives shall have intervened.

Although much of the text of these two documents deals with practical matters, it's clear that at least some spiritual principles were written into them, particularly the Declaration. The Founders and Framers based the Declaration and Constitution on human nature. It's important to understand that human nature isn't fixed; it evolves slowly, it's evolved over time, and it's still evolving. We have the capacity to affect our nature by conscious choice. We have the capacity to grow into human beings with a spiritual perspective. Once we accomplish this, we're better able to focus on all the things we have in common as our foundation. From that, we learn to work together and eventually create a world that is at peace; a world in which each person takes responsibility for their life and their actions and acts for the highest good of all.

It's also quite clear the Founders and Framers chose to protect individual and State rights and to limit the scope of the Federal government. They designed a Federal government to oversee specific aspects of operating our country, leaving the rest to the State governments. (The term Federal refers to a *confederation* of States with each State retaining some autonomy.) Some attendees of the Philadelphia Convention presented the idea of a National government, which is what our government has essentially grown into. (A National government, as you probably surmised, has most of the power invested into a central government with limited powers retained by the States.) Although it had some proponents at the Convention, a National form of government was ultimately rejected as too powerful. Many people feared the government would use its power to control too much of their lives (that thought may seem familiar to many of today's Americans).

Comparing what the Framers intended to our current government shows how far we have strayed from our founding and how far away we have come from the independent spirit of our forefathers. Our forefathers demanded liberty; over time we've collectively abdicated much of our liberty and settled for a weak promise of illusory security, for which we've paid an exorbitant price.

In the next chapter I'll describe the foundation of a spiritual Republic: true spirituality. A spiritual Republic becomes truly possible once a majority of its citizens have true spiritual principles as their moral foundation

Part Three: What is Spirituality, and Why Should You Believe What I Say?

The information in this section is vitally important to deeply understanding the nature of a spiritual Republic. Understanding spirituality is essential for our society to be able to develop into a spiritual Republic. This section provides the background information necessary to understanding the perspectives presented in upcoming chapters.

People have different ideas about the meaning of spirituality. I'll be sharing my ideas on this so you know where I'm coming from. I want everyone reading this book to understand this foundation so you'll know exactly what I mean and can decide for yourself if these ideas make sense to you.

I'm also going to work on giving you reasons to trust me. There is precious little trust in this world, and it's often withheld for good reasons. While there will be things I tell you that I can't directly prove, I'll be providing a consistent message with as much verification as I can. I want to earn your trust so what I'm presenting has more credibility. I'm asking you to give me the benefit of the doubt and a chance to explain these perspectives. Changing your point of view will help to improve your life, the lives of people around you, our country, and our world.

There is one other reason I'm presenting this information in this book, and it's really the most important reason to include this section. I know that the key to successfully reaching a spiritual Republic is dependent upon more and more people in the United States genuinely becoming more spiritual. Only with a solid spiritual foundation, and without the pitfalls of our current lifestyles and government, can we hope to achieve the greatness that is possible for America.

Before we start, I'd like to ask you to keep an open mind. Some of these ideas may contradict some things you already believe. If that's the case, simply pretend you're reading a novel and "suspend your disbelief." If you at least give these ideas a chance, you may find they make more sense than you thought they would, or they're not really that different from what you already believe.

Please keep in mind that this won't be an in-depth exploration of spirituality. I'll be covering some of the key principles, so, if you're ready, let's take a closer look at the meaning behind *spirituality*.

Spirituality

Spirituality deals with things we believe in but mostly don't see and can't directly prove. Despite that, many people believe spiritual principles are real, and these principles are things that are common to most religions in the world.

Most of these principles will be familiar to you. The description may be a little different than what you're accustomed to, but the core message is likely to be one you already know. Here are what I believe to be some of the most important spiritual principles:

- **God and angels exist, and they're here to help us in our everyday lives.**

No one can directly *prove* either God or angels exist. That means you have the choice of disbelieving or taking this one on faith (at least until you have your own experiences to verify this – which you may have already). If you believe this is true, then that means we are not in this alone and we have great resources working *for* us, even if every human in the world lets us down – and that could include yourself. One thing to keep in mind: if you ask for help, be completely open to how that help may turn up, and *accept it when it does come*.

- **You are responsible for your actions.**

What you do *matters*. The things you do and the things you choose affect you and other people. Therefore, anything you do that causes a problem or hurts someone, including yourself, has to be made right. And it's up to you to fix the situation.

- **You are responsible for your life and what's in it.**

Your life is the sum of your choices and the actions you take, plus the choices others make that directly affect you. In every case, you are responsible for your choices and their consequences. Plus, you're responsible for how you act and react to things that happen around you. From this point of view, it's easy to see that each of us has more potential control over our lives than we realize or exercise. If you don't like things as they are in your life, make new decisions, take new actions, and make new choices that support those changes.

- **It's important to make right choices and to not make negative or bad choices.**

Most of us have a very good grasp of the difference between right and wrong. This world makes it easy to make negative choices and to choose to do the wrong thing. However, just because others do the wrong thing doesn't mean *you* have to. Since you already make many right choices, why not start now to make most or all of your choices right? There's no downside to this, and every one of us has respect for people who tell the truth and no respect for liars. Plus, consistently making right choices and telling the truth speeds up our spiritual growth, while lying and making negative choices makes spiritual growth much harder.

- **Accept the things that happen in your life with grace, and work on improving what you can.**

Things are going to happen that you don't like. Your spiritual perspective can strongly affect how you react to difficult times. When you react calmly and with grace, you experience less stress and your mind stays clear. You're better able to assess your options and determine the best course of action. This is something we *all* want to have working for us.

- **Love the people close to you and have good will toward everyone else.**

The best way to love the people closest to you is *unconditionally* – love freely given without limits or conditions. Having good will toward others includes treating them with courtesy and kindness.

- **Treat yourself and others with respect.**

Many people in our society, especially youth, seem to lack self-respect and respect for others. There are a number of problems with this. Lack of respect often leads to a lack of common courtesy, a tendency to disregard the hurt we cause (to ourselves and others), and often leads to negative behaviors, such as addictions (alcohol, drugs, gambling, and other negative behaviors), bullying in different forms, and even criminal behavior (including theft, robbery, and assault).

- **Honesty and integrity are important.**

Despite what some people seem to believe, honesty and integrity are still important in today's society – perhaps more important than ever before. It's much easier to have a peaceful heart and clear conscience if you are honest and live your life decently. These two values are essential to developing a deep and truly spiritual perspective.

- **It's best to not make judgments about others.**

Simply put, making judgments limits your thinking and your perspective. And, to top it off, those judgments are often wrong. Since you won't ever know everything motivating someone's actions, you'll always be missing some information, and there's no way you can make an accurate assessment without some or all of the facts. Making judgments is a form of negative thinking, and negative thinking hurts your spiritual growth.

- **Recognize that others have their own point of view and respect that – even if you don't agree.**

Everyone is a composite of different experiences and perceptions. No two of us are exactly alike. Therefore, none of us are likely to agree with someone else about *everything*. The hardest part of this is feeling as though you're absolutely right, wanting to be proven right, and wanting others to be right too – by embracing your point of view. It's important to remember that your point of view suits you fine, but it isn't necessarily right for everyone else. Similarly, someone else's point of view could be all wrong for you. So accept other people's perspectives as right for them and let it be.

- **How we treat our planet and environment is very important because what we do affects *all* future generations.**

Unless we really screw up, we're not the last generation that will be living on this Earth. However, we've done a great job at leaving a screwed up Earth to future generations (The Founders and Framers called this "posterity.") Since many of us still here today are in part responsible for this, we need to take responsibility and not leave the cleanup to our children and grandchildren. We may not finish the job on our watch, but we have the responsibility of doing everything we can to fix this before we're gone. Taking responsibility is a necessary part of having a spiritual perspective. Now that I've shared some of the basic principles, let's look at some of the myths and truths of spirituality.

Myths and Truths of Spirituality

For some people, the concept of a "spiritual" person evokes an image of isolation – being separate from the world in order to pursue a spiritual path. These ideas often take the form of a hermit in a cave, a monk behind the walls of a monastery, or, from our past, the American hippie separating from "regular" society. While these have all been used in the past, these concepts no longer apply to today's world.

In today's world, *our day to day life is our spiritual life*. This means our day to day "self" is the person who can live a spiritual life. Living a spiritual life doesn't require waiting for things to be "right." It doesn't happen "some day." Your spiritual life can start **today,** with things in your life exactly as they are. You only need to do one thing for this to happen, and that is to *make the choice.*

Decide that *right now* is the beginning of your true spiritual life and act as though it were already true and cannot change. Perhaps you've already made this choice. If so, thank you for taking responsibility for your growth and for making the world a better place. Now, let's take a closer look at a few specific spiritual myths. We'll start with one that is often misunderstood.

Myth: A spiritual person cannot and will not use violence against another person for any reason.
This myth seems on the surface to be "right." But there are two strong errors in this statement. Making this specific choice goes against the spiritual principle of self-responsibility and the natural law of self-defense.

The truth behind this is that a spiritual person will not, under any circumstances, *perpetrate **unnecessary** violence* against another person. Let's look at this a bit more in depth and consider a specific example.

If, as a spiritual person, you become the victim of a violent crime, following this myth takes away all of your choices *and* your self-responsibility for your well being. This goes directly against the spiritual principle of *self-responsibility*. By making this choice, you've abdicated your personal responsibility and given it to the violent criminal. You've decided to make them responsible for you, and that is absolutely not a true spiritual perspective.

With a true spiritual perspective, you know you are ultimately responsible for your own well-being. Therefore, a true spiritual perspective won't permit you to give up that self-responsibility and give it to someone else – especially a violent criminal. This also goes against the natural law of self-protection. According to the spiritually–based laws of Nature, you and every form of life on Earth has the right to protect that life.

Most people who believe this myth at a spiritual level aren't in fact making a spiritual decision. This decision is nearly always based on fear. Making the choice to never, under any circumstances, use violence against another person is simply the easy way out. It's a handy excuse for being able to mentally avoid something you don't ever want to face. And this is completely understandable.

As civilized people, the idea of severely injuring or even killing someone is reprehensible. However, there are circumstances under which it may become *necessary*. Let's look at a specific example.

Suppose you're a parent or grandparent, and a criminal grabs your child and begins to beat or stab them, and may even be trying to kill them. Following this myth, all you can "do" is to either plead with them or just stand by and watch. Pleading is clearly not going to work, and we'd be willing to bet that *no one* reading this would choose to stand by and do nothing while their child is being maimed or killed. *Every* parent or grandparent would take action, and that action will include whatever is necessary to stop the attacker – even if stopping that attacker results in their death.

So, is protecting your child a "non-spiritual" point of view? Absolutely not! In fact, *not* protecting them would be a non-spiritual perspective. Even if your actions ultimately result in the death of the attacker, it's important to realize that the attacker placed you in that position, and the outcome was due to *their own actions. Therefore, the situation is entirely their responsibility.*

The attacker set these events in motion, and the attacker decided how far you had to go. They had the choice to not perpetrate the crime, and they could have stopped at any point. Stopping the crime, by whatever means necessary, is the **spiritual** thing to do.

If we continue this line of thinking, it's easy to see that the natural right to self-protection and the spiritual principle of self-responsibility both support Second Amendment rights, and both also include the right of a true spiritual Republic to defend its citizens and itself from those who would choose to tear it down and destroy it.

This means that a spiritual Republic would have a very powerful military for its own protection. A spiritual Republic would never use that power for conquest, but, as we already know, a Republic of this type is a target for other forces in the world that already do not wish us well and are bent on our destruction. While those others have the right to live their lives as they choose to, they do **not** have the right to try and destroy our nation and way of life.

Incidentally, the Founders and Framers recognized that one of the best ways to ensure peace and deter aggressors is to be a powerful nation. Here are a few examples from historical documents. The first is from George Washington's State of the Union address on January 8, 1790. In this excerpt, you'll see how necessary George Washington believed it was for the country to be ready for war at all times:

> "Among the many interesting objects which will engage your attention that of providing for the common defense will merit particular regard. To be prepared for war is one of the most effectual means of preserving peace.
>
> A free people ought not only to be armed, but disciplined; to which end a uniform and well-digested plan is requisite; and their safety and interest require that they should promote such manufactories as tend to render them independent of others for essential, particularly military, supplies."

And this by John Jay, from the Federalist Papers #4:

"But whatever may be our situation, whether firmly united under one national government, or split into a number of confederacies, certain it is that foreign nations will know and view it exactly as it is; and they will act toward us accordingly. If they see that our national government is efficient and well administered, our trade prudently regulated, our militia properly organized and disciplined, our resources and finances discreetly managed, our credit re-established, our people free, contented, and united, they will be much more disposed to cultivate our friendship than provoke our resentment."

And lastly, from Thomas Jefferson's 8th Annual message in 1808:
"For a people who are free and who mean to remain so, a well-organized and armed militia is their best security. It is, therefore, incumbent on us at every meeting [of Congress] to revise the condition of the militia and to ask ourselves if it is prepared to repel a powerful enemy at every point of our territories exposed to invasion... Congress alone have power to produce a uniform state of preparation in this great organ of defense. The interests which they so deeply feel in their own and their country's security will present this as among the most important objects of their deliberation."

Myth: I have to be passive and (almost) perfect to be a deeply spiritual person.
Living according to spiritual principles becomes your way of life. However, there are *many* options for living a spiritual life in today's world. You can live the life you choose, and that life is your spiritual life. Fortunately, your chosen spiritual lifestyle doesn't require perfection or for you to sit idly on the sidelines.

You're still a person in a physical body, so it's completely OK to have preferences. It's OK to like some things or people and not others. It's even OK to be wrong now and then. Some of the attributes you'll find helpful as a spiritual person in today's society are: humility, acceptance, courtesy, patience, and a flexible perspective. Perfection isn't necessary, and that's why it's not on this list.

As a deeply spiritual person, you will hold yourself to a higher standard. However, that standard won't be perfection because it's exceedingly difficult to be perfect in a physical world, and perfection is *not* required of anyone, including people with a spiritual perspective.

This is the bottom line: you're on the right track if you're humble, accept that others are free to make their own choices about their lives, and look for an opportunity to spiritually grow in every situation. Now let's take a short look at the idea that a spiritual life is a *passive* life.

Spirituality is not about sitting around and waiting for things to happen. It's about understanding our true nature, the true nature of the world around us, and what we can learn from the things that happen around us. A deep spiritual life comes from being *immersed* in life. It comes from interacting with other people; it comes from experiencing many things in this world and learning from them; it comes from *truly* plugging in on a physical level (and absolutely NOT living your life inside a 2 inch screen!).

In a sense, a truly spiritual life has to be experienced and can't be lived out of books. Therefore, living your life completely passively *can't truly be* a spiritual life. So if you're worried that you'll need to be a hermit and leave your family for a cozy little cave, you can let that worry go. You can develop a spiritual life from the life you are living *right now.* You don't need to leave anyone behind, you don't have to give up your comfortable home, and you can still be yourself.

Myth: A deeply spiritual person lives an austere life and is spiritually required to be poor.
When most of us think about the people who are historically considered spiritual, we see that most of them have been poor. Plus, somewhere in the Bible it says "For the love of money is the root of all kinds of evil." Those are a couple of big strikes against spirituality in today's society. However, looking at this more closely, it's apparent that it's the *person,* and not the *money,* that is the problem.

What that quote essentially says is "Don't be greedy." Now, that's perfectly good spiritual advice, and anyone with a deeply spiritual perspective will completely agree. The quote does not in any way say "Don't have money." You can have all the money you want, as long as you use it without greed. It really is that simple.

The first of two words of caution: In a spiritual sense, caring about everything around you includes not wasting resources. That's why many people with a deeply spiritual perspective are often frugal. You can have as many resources as you wish; just be willing to use them wisely and not waste them.

The other word of caution is this: you must acquire those resources *ethically*. This means that your conduct, whether as an employee or a business owner, must be ethical. If not, your resources won't be spiritually earned and you will quickly succumb to greed.

There is no spiritual reason you can't have abundance. In fact, our true spiritual nature *is* abundant, so following a spiritual path can lead to prosperity. You can have a large house or anything else you want if you have a useful purpose for it, and if you acquire your wealth in accordance with spiritual principles.

Now that we've looked at a few myths and their truths, let's explore the idea of spiritual Laws.

Some essential Spiritual Laws

Many different authors have named a number of different spiritual laws. We'll take a brief look at six spiritual Laws that are fundamental to our life and existence. They may not be the only spiritual laws that exist, but these six are an important part of our daily lives.

The Universal Law of Balance

Balance is an essential part of everything in our universe. Everything works toward balance; toward equilibrium. All of our body's functions need balance for us to have optimal wellness. Our Earth remains where it is and remains habitable due to the balance between the sun's gravity and the earth's orbital momentum. Even our purchasing or barter transactions seek balance.

Balance is important spiritually as well. Spiritual imbalances often lead to negative choices and sometimes even erratic behavior. This stems from the imbalance causing a form of energy "pressure" that's trying to become balanced again. Our ego interprets this pressure as a problem in our lives, but this perception is distorted because the ego can't perceive the spiritual cause of the imbalance. Therefore, it tries to make physical changes to correct a spiritual problem, and this generally doesn't work.

As we grow spiritually, we become better able to perceive any spiritual imbalances we create, and we learn to resolve them spiritually. This properly restores the balance without adding much stress or strain to our lives.

The Universal Law of Cause and Effect
The essence of this law is simple: actions have consequences. Those consequences often lead to more consequences as the effects of our actions ripple out. This is one of the main reasons it's spiritually best to choose actions that are for the highest good of all. It's far better to have positive consequences rippling out, benefiting many others, than to have negative consequences rippling out and harming many others.

The Universal Law of Free Will
Most of us are already familiar with this one. This natural law gives us our right to *choose*. This is obviously a double-edged sword. We are free to make choices, but we must also accept the consequences of those choices. We are directly responsible for the outcome of our choices, and societies that take away a law-abiding person's right to choose violate the spiritual principle of self-responsibility, which is a component of the spiritual law of free will.

The Universal Law of Manifestation
This is the essence of this spiritual law: What you focus your intention on that is for your spiritual benefit, and then take action to achieve, will manifest. We do this all the time, mainly without thinking about it. And some of you reading this will have done these exact steps without achieving your intended result. There are several reasons why this happens.

One of the main reasons is that we often want things that aren't in our best spiritual interest. In those cases, we apply the Law of Manifestation without any result because our Higher Self (more about this in a couple of pages) intervenes and stops the process from working. Other times, the process works and we get the result we want. We generally get a mixed bag of results because our Higher Self stops the process when it's not in our best interest, but it does allow things to manifest (both positive and negative) that are necessary to our spiritual growth.

The Universal Law of Harmlessness
Many of us violate this law every day. The essence of this law is that we should do no harm to anyone else or the world around us. The spiritual benefits that come from following this law are many. When we follow it, we're consciously aware of all the effects of our actions so we only take actions that provide a positive outcome – both physically and spiritually. As a result, we're constantly doing the right thing at the right time and we accelerate our spiritual growth. We do a lot of good things for the people we interact with every day when our actions conform to this spiritual law.

The Universal Law of Experience
This law simply states that we have to experience everything we create. Experiencing everything we create ensures that we experience the results of our actions; we're not exempt from them, so we need to take actions that result in positive outcomes and the highest good for all. We all know of people who make decisions for others (like some politicians and business managers) who don't have to live with the immediate consequences of their decisions. For some people, it's easy to make a decision that will negatively affect others if that negative affect doesn't apply to them. Unfortunately, that is a short-sighted decision since they will eventually have to experience the harm they've caused.

The importance of spiritual awareness
The degree of your spiritual awareness directly affects your perceptions, perspectives, and actions. This means what you perceive, how you view things, and what you do are all affected by what level of spiritual awareness you have.

Since this is really important, we'll take a short look at some of the different "levels" of spiritual awareness. Each further step deepens honesty, integrity, truthfulness, and trustworthiness. I'll tell you a bit more about this as we address each level. Let's take a look at the stages of spiritual awareness.

The stages of spiritual awareness

Everyone you meet is at some point on the spiritual continuum. This can range from completely spiritually unaware up to spiritual mastery and beyond. I'll describe some of these basic stages and will be referencing these stages frequently throughout the remainder of this book. First we'll look at the "average" person out on the street. Remember that these stages are broad strokes and may not specifically describe you or anyone you know.

The "average" person who is *spiritually unaware*

Most people on Earth fit into this category. Their emotional, mental, and spiritual focus is their personal sense of self. They believe they are separate from the world and everyone in it. Events may seem random, and most people in this state believe in some sort of punitive God. Most people in this state don't fully understand that the consequences of their actions affect their lives and the lives of people around them. They're typically not very good at taking responsibility for their actions.

They get a few spiritual communications now and then; what we call "intuition." Their personal sense of self, or ego, is all they really know and all they believe they can rely on since other people will sometimes help them and sometimes not. From this point of view, the world seems random and often cruel.

This perspective serves an important spiritual purpose, and there are specific spiritual reasons people in this state feel the way they feel and act the way they act. I'll briefly explain these reasons and show you a diagram that may help.

It turns out that, in our true spiritual form, we have vast knowledge and tremendous awareness. Having this much awareness makes it hard to learn and grow spiritually – which is something we are all here to do. So, we have a "curtain" between our spiritual self and our individual "sense" of self, or our ego. This curtain is called the *veil*.

The veil separates our ego from the part of our true spiritual self that comes here to Earth. You've heard of that part, because that part is our *soul*. In this next diagram, you'll see this called our "manifested soul." That's because the soul is only a part of our true spiritual self. The other, and larger, part of our spiritual self is called the "Higher Self." This is the part of us that has vast knowledge and tremendous awareness. Its knowledge and awareness is kept from our ego and mind by the curtain, or veil.

Let's take a look at that diagram:

The "average" person:

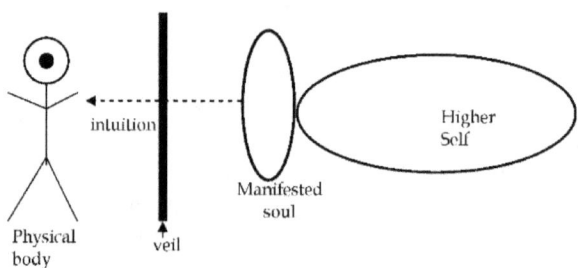

As you can see from this diagram, the physical body and the soul have a block between them that stops open communication. A bit of intuition gets through, but that's about it. Our soul is still a part of us, but it's the part that lives on spiritual planes we can't perceive with our five senses. You'll see the larger part of our spiritual self, our Higher Self, is in connection with our soul.

Having that block, or veil, changes things a lot. Spiritually, our ego is supposed to be a messenger between our physical body and our soul. With the block in place, the ego has to assume control, but it's not designed for that. It's out of its element, and things generally look scary and unpredictable. However, growing spiritually begins to solve this problem. Our point of view changes, what we perceive changes, and our actions change too. That brings us to the next step: *spiritually open*.

Someone who is *spiritually open*
In this next diagram, we'll see a few changes occurring. The block, or veil, gets thinner, and allows more intuition through. As the veil

gets thinner, your point of view changes, what you perceive changes, and what you do changes.

In this state, it becomes clear that we are all a part of something bigger. We recognize that there is a deeper order to things that we don't often perceive. We know we're connected in some way to the people around us, to the world around us, and possibly even people we don't know. We're beginning to understand the real meaning of "actions have consequences."

Someone who is spiritually open knows that they're responsible for what they do. They know that bad choices generally have bad outcomes, and it's possible to avoid at least some of those bad outcomes by making better choices. They're beginning to see that honesty and integrity are important. They know that other people may believe different things, but their opinions are their own and it's OK if they're different. People at this level are more accepting and tolerant.

While not perfect, people who are spiritually open are generally calmer, more forgiving, and more accepting. They still have their ego in charge of their actions, but the context has changed since they recognize there is more to the world than they perceive. They're also more accepting of change and comfortable with change.

Let's take a look at the diagram for being *spiritually open:*

Spiritually open:

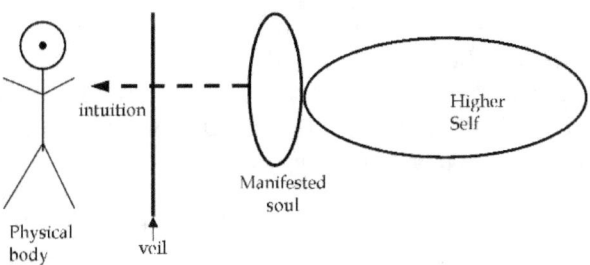

In this diagram you'll see that the veil is thinner. The thinner veil allows more spiritual communications to come through, such as more intuition and more information from our soul. This is more important than it may seem since it's the thinning veil that helps us deepen our awareness and spiritual understanding.

Now let's look at the next step: being *spiritually awake*.

Someone who is *spiritually awake*

Things really change once someone becomes spiritually awake. The veil drops away at this level, and spiritual understanding takes a big step forward. The most important change happens after the veil drops, and that is when *your soul takes control of your personal self instead of your ego being in charge.*

When this happens, it not like you become someone else. You're beginning to become your true spiritual self. As we mentioned before, the ego is supposed to be a messenger between your soul and physical body. It takes the spiritual messages from your soul and translates them into physical action. It's doing the job it was designed to do so it's much happier.

Someone who is spiritually awake no longer has the veil to conceal their true spiritual nature. It's much easier to understand that we truly are spiritual beings without the veil in place. And, as spiritual beings, we can genuinely *feel* that we are connected to this Universe and everything in it. We also feel as though we're on a cusp; that, at any moment, we will burst into clarity and everything will make much more sense. We know we have a purpose, and we know each of us has a unique purpose.

With your soul in control of your physical body, the negative behaviors you may have had in the past no longer exert much influence on you. By choice, you do what you know and feel is right. While you're not perfect, you'll make fewer errors, feel more balanced, whole, and calm, and you'll value honesty and integrity even more than you did when spiritually open.

As may be apparent, someone at this level is very truthful and trustworthy. They'll be far less likely – in fact, very unlikely – to engage in negative behaviors like lying, dishonesty, cheating, being driven by greed, hurting others, and many other negative choices that are so much a part of our lives when the ego is in control.

That's because those behaviors come from the ego, and the soul will not engage in them.

Let's take a look at the diagram for someone who is spiritually awake:

Spiritually awake:

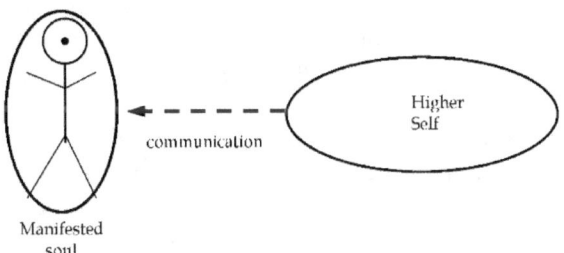

As you can see, the manifested soul is now in full control of the physical body. Without the veil, there is nothing in place to interfere with the connection to the Higher Self. While there is nothing blocking this connection, it still needs to be fully activated and opened. This comes in time, and is a part of the next step in our spiritual growth: the beginning of spiritual mastery.

The beginning of spiritual mastery

Spiritual mastery is rarely spoken of. I believe this is in part due to a lack of true understanding about spiritual mastery. Spiritual mastery is *not* mastering people around you or asserting your will over the world. True spiritual mastery is *self* mastery.

A spiritual master has worked through all the levels we've covered. A spiritual master still has an ego, but the ego is in its proper place functioning as a messenger between the soul and the physical body. The soul is in complete control over the body. Please note that this *doesn't* mean your physical body suddenly becomes perfect. It's still physical, it's still in the world, and it's still subject to the laws of physics.

A spiritual master has a vastly different perspective compared to the average person. As a result, the spiritual master makes very different choices. Where an "average" person may think it's OK for a clerk at a large store to make a mistake in your favor, a spiritual master will absolutely not, and is spiritually compelled to bring that error to the clerk's attention. Cheat a bit on your taxes? A spiritual master will not – by choice.

Also by choice, a spiritual master will not lie, steal, perpetrate harm against others, or engage in any other harmful behaviors. A spiritual master is relentlessly honest, and values their integrity as much as their life. Absolute truthfulness is essential. As such, a spiritual master is virtually incorruptible – even if they were in a place like Washington, D.C..

A spiritual master also has access to an enormous storehouse of information in the spiritual worlds. This means that they often learn things directly through their spiritual connection. That connection is with their Higher Self, and, as we mentioned before, the Higher Self has enormous knowledge – which is why we needed the veil in the first place. Let's take a look at the diagram for spiritual mastery:

The beginning of spiritual mastery:

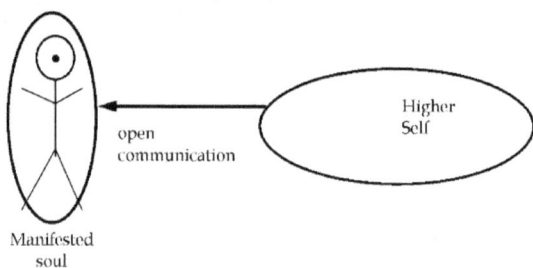

As you can see, there is no veil, the soul is in control, and there is open communication between the manifested soul and the Higher Self. The open communication channels carry information and much more.

One other important point I want to mention is this: spiritual mastery as I've outlined it here is *very* attainable. Some focused work educating ourselves spiritually and growing our perspectives gets us off to a good start. In this case, a little guidance can go a long way as well. To be truly effective, that guidance will need to come from someone who has reached the level of spiritual mastery.

As you might imagine, having a government of statesmen who are spiritually awake or at the beginnings of spiritual mastery would be vastly superior to our current government. The drive for power would essentially be gone. Greed wouldn't be a factor either. The choices such representatives made would be according to the will of the people, constitutionally correct, and structured in a way that would provide the highest good for all. Peace, courtesy, and prosperity would become a genuine way of life for all American citizens.

I mentioned the ego a number of times in the past section, and I'd like to take a closer look at the ego's purpose and the way it works.

A bit about the ego

The ego's proper function is to act as a messenger between your soul and physical body. Let's look at what the ego actually is, and how its process of making decisions differs from how the soul makes decisions.

Most people perceive the ego as their individual sense of self. It's generally perceived as being in our head because that's where our major sense organs and brain are located. This sense of self creates our feeling of individuality, and, as individuals, it's why we feel separate from the world and everyone around us. This changes once our ego comes into constant communication with our soul.

Once our ego begins to communicate with our soul, we begin to feel as though there is more to the world than we've seen so far. This marks the beginning of our spiritual journey. Our point of view expands even further as we progress on our journey and our soul is in even more contact with our ego. This is the process of the soul beginning to assume control over our physical body.

There is also a difference in how the ego approaches decisions and how the soul approaches them. The ego is generally selfish in its decision making process. When considering its options, the ego most often chooses what will benefit itself most, OR what will cause it the least amount of pain and discomfort. The soul, on the other hand, makes the choice that brings the most overall benefit into the situation – for itself and for others. Unpleasant decisions are made without regard to personal pain and discomfort, and the soul will always make the choice that brings the highest spiritual outcome and the greatest benefit to everyone involved.

You've probably noticed that some people you meet seem to have a "lot" of ego, while some have less. I created some simple diagrams to help explain the relative "strength" of the ego and what the general ramifications are of each level of ego. A dot (in the stick man's head) represents the ego in these diagrams, and these diagrams all represent the "average person" who is generally not yet spiritually open.

Before we get into the diagrams, I'd like to mention one key point: your soul influences your ego as long as there is some degree of communication between your soul and your ego. What this means is that your soul influence moderates the ego and, to at least some degree, keeps the ego in check. This has an important affect on our behavior and choices. Let's start with the ego of the "average" person.

The "average" person with a "normal" amount of ego generally makes a blend of choices. Many of their choices take other people into account, but some do not. A little bit of dishonesty can creep in, commonly in mistakes that work out in their favor with large businesses. They rationalize this as "no one really got hurt." The "average" ego cares about others, but generally cares more about itself. Let's look at the diagram for a person with an "average" ego:

The "average" person:

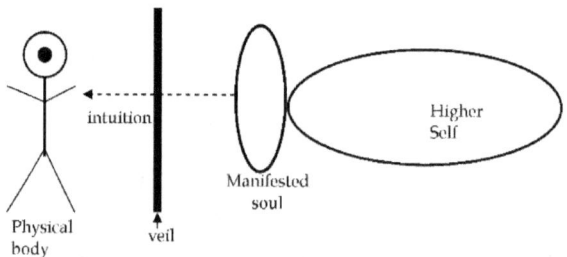

The "average" person with an ego of "average" relative strength. Some contact from the person's soul through intuition moderates the ego and helps to keep it partially in check.

Now let's consider someone we'd view as a "really good" person. This is someone who is still not yet spiritually open, but who spends much of their time helping others and doing things to help other people. In their case the ego has a lower relative "strength" than the ego of the average person. They tend to receive more communications from their soul so their ego is kept more in check by their soul as compared to an "average" person. Here is the diagram for a "really good" person who is not yet spiritually aware:

The "really good" person:

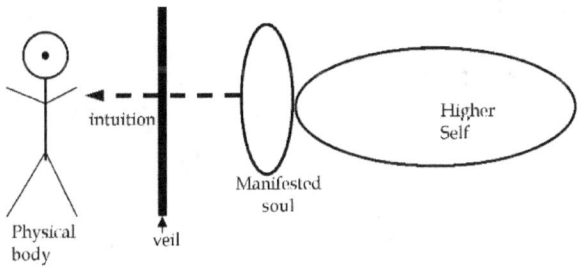

In this diagram, the dot that represents the relative "strength" of the ego is smaller than for an "average" person. Also note that there is more influence from the person's soul through increased intuition. Since the soul moderates the ego, greater communication from the soul through intuition is what led to a weaker ego.

Now let's consider someone "really bad." In their case they have no real communication from their soul, so their soul exerts almost no moderating influence in the ego. Their ego runs rampant because of this. They tend to have very little self-control, and often exhibit destructive behaviors. As you'll see in the diagram, such a person is essentially cut off from spiritual influence and is completely under control of their ego. Here is the diagram:

The "really bad" person:

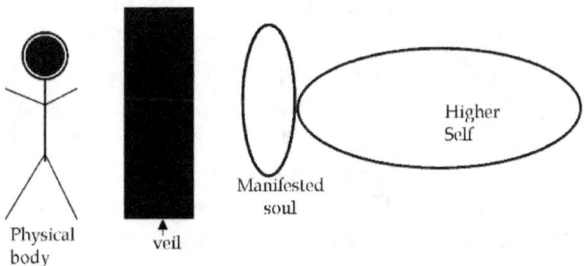

As you can see in this diagram, the veil is so thick that the person has no contact with their manifested soul. The ego has run unchecked and is out of control. The person's actions will likewise tend to be out of control — unless they have an exceptionally strong stabilizing and loving influence in their lives.

As you can see from the previous discussion, there are various spiritual reasons why people can be very different, even if they have a number of things in common. In this book I obviously can't describe a situation to explain every circumstance, but I hope I've at least provided enough information to make this understandable.

Spiritual awareness and trustworthiness

There is a direct correlation between increasing spiritual awareness and increasing trustworthiness. The cause of this is also quite direct.

All of the "negative" behaviors, such as stealing, deceit, manipulations, robbery, assault, and all the other ways to hurt other people are only used by the ego. That's why some people who we'd consider "really bad" do many "bad" things, and do them often. They have no moderating communication from their soul to keep their ego in check. Conversely, someone who is spiritually open or awake has more moderating communication from their soul (since their veil is thinner or lifted) so they'll naturally choose to do fewer negative and hurtful things. They'll more often make choices that help other people, along with helping themselves.

It really is that simple. The soul has no reason to use negative behaviors so it doesn't. As we grow spiritually, our awareness deepens, our connection with our soul deepens, and we make more positive choices.

This brings up one last point on this topic: what exactly *is* trustworthiness? How can a person tell if someone else is *trustworthy?*

I think the answer to this is fairly straightforward. People who are trustworthy have a high degree of correlation between their words and their deeds. This consistency won't waver; it comes from deep inside them and it comes from their sense of personal integrity. Anyone who says one thing and does another is *not* trustworthy (an example we see from many politicians). Such a person has a hidden agenda and is telling people what they want to hear in order to get their support (or their money). When you're focusing on spiritual growth, it's best to surround yourself with trustworthy people and to keep away from those who aren't. Naturally, it's also best to *be* trustworthy yourself.

What makes a perspective *spiritual?*

We've covered a lot of foundational spiritual principles, and I've even mentioned having a spiritual "point of view." It's about time to focus on what that means.

Let's look at this as a comparison. Let's compare an "average" person's perspective with a "spiritual" perspective. An average person sees a world that is completely apart from them. It's a world that is often harsh and hostile. It's an uncaring world filled with random events – some of which work in their favor, but more that don't. People close to them may care about them, at least to some degree, but no one else really seems to.

Many people in the world seem to be out for themselves, rather than trying to make a positive difference or trying to make the world a better place. This person can see that some do try, but it seems like fighting the tide; it seems too hopeless to even bother. In this world, it boils down mainly to luck – good luck, bad luck, and being in the right or wrong place at the right or wrong time.

Now let's shift gears. Let's see the same world through the lens of a spiritual perspective.

A spiritual person sees a world outside of them, but it's a world that they fit into, and in which they have a purpose. They know that bad things will happen, but those bad things are often the result of their own or another person's negative choices and they're not caused randomly by "the world" at all. Since they're aware of this, they know that their actions have consequences, and those consequences often affect other people as well. They know that the people around them, even when they choose to do negative things, are still spiritual beings at their core – and that means their true self is a radiant, loving, caring being.

Even though many people are trying to get ahead at the expense of others, a spiritual person will seek and find solutions that allow for personal choice by everyone involved and bring the highest good possible. The spiritual person sees that the world is formed by our choices, so they'll make the best choices possible and are an example for others. The spiritual person knows there is more to the world than our eyes and other senses show us, and they know the unseen part of the world and ourselves is truly the greater and more important part of us.

As you can see, the "average" person as depicted above lives in a very different world than the spiritual person depicted. It's pretty clear which world is easier to live in, and which leads to more good things. And while both of these are simply descriptions on this page, both represent realities that many people live in. These are realities that each of us choose every day.

Some people reading these paragraphs may come to the conclusion that each of us is somehow in charge of *all* reality since our choices, from this point of view, seem to entirely create our reality and future. Fortunately, this is not at all the case.

Even though our choices shape our present and future, it's important to recognize that our choices aren't written onto an entirely blank page. In addition to the consequences of our actions, there is a "framework" that our choices fit into. It's just like writing our thoughts down on paper.

When we write, we change the paper and it's meaning by adding ink that forms ideas and thoughts. However, *we didn't make the paper or put lines on it.* We used the paper as it was, with the lines already there. That's the way our choices work spiritually – we put them out there and those choices lead to consequences. Those consequences then come into being according to the spiritual principles that operate our world – and those principles are like the paper and lines. Those principles create the framework, so it's important to know that the consequences from our choices aren't random and don't come out of a vacuum. They're a part of the spiritual principle of *cause and effect.*

Now let's take a brief look at religion.

Religion, *religions,* and spirituality

As you've already seen, the foundational principles of spirituality and what most of us mean when we say "religion" are essentially the same. That's because they *are* the same at their root. The confusion about differentiating religion from spirituality comes about from confusing *religion* with *religious organizations.*

Spirituality and *religious organizations* are absolutely NOT the same. We know that spirituality deals with things we believe in but mostly don't see and can't prove. Religious organizations, on the other hand, are all about *people*. There are people of all levels of spiritual understanding in almost all religious organizations. That means there are people who are wise – and there are people who are corruptible and out for personal power or prestige.

The strength of any religious organization is limited by the strength and spiritual awareness of its members. Knowing this, it's easy to see how some organizations seem to operate in a more positive way than others. Fortunately, every single one of us can begin today to live our lives according to spiritual principles, regardless of what religious organization we may be a part of (if any).

As spiritual beings, we're not limited by the perspectives of any organization, and we've already seen that the roots of spirituality exist in all religions. What we do with those principles is truly our own choice, regardless of what the organization may want us to do.

The next topic in our introduction to spiritual principles is a specific spiritual faculty that you're familiar with: *intuition*.

Intuition
The reason I want to bring up intuition is precisely *because* everyone is familiar with it. I mentioned intuition before, and you may have noticed it on the spiritual awareness diagrams. Let's expand our thoughts about intuition a bit so you may be able to see it in a more spiritual light.

In essence, most instances of intuition are a *basic form of spiritual communication*. Since it's something all of us have, accepting this idea makes it easy to see that we all, already, use a basic form of spiritual communication. So where does intuition come from?

Some instances of intuition come from stored information in our subconscious mind – but not *all* instances of intuition are from the subconscious mind. Many originate in the *superconscious mind –* which is the Higher Self. You may remember seeing the Higher Self on the spiritual awareness charts as well. If you refer back to those charts (on pages 72 to 76), you'll see dashed lines that cross the veil, and those lines represent intuitive communication from your Higher Self to your conscious mind.

If you even *think* this could be correct, then you'll easily realize – and possibly accept – that this type of spiritual communication is already a part of your life and nearly everyone else's. Accepting this is a great place to start from to begin the process of deepening your spiritual awareness.

Interestingly, imagination works much the same way as intuition, and is also a great tool to help deepen your spiritual awareness.

Now let's take a brief look at how deepening your spiritual awareness can improve your life – and even the world.

Spiritual awareness in everyday life

Some readers may be wondering why we should bother with this at all. What are the benefits in everyday life, if any, from having a deeper spiritual awareness? This is a fair question, and we looked at this just a bit in a previous section about what makes a perspective spiritual. Now we'll dig in a bit deeper.

You saw an obvious difference in the two ways of looking at the world that I outlined, but I need to tell you *why* that difference is there. At its very root, deeper spiritual understanding leads to an inner calmness, peace, and sense of purpose that isn't possible without true spiritual awareness. The most obvious benefit of this inner peace is this: the stress is either greatly reduced or fundamentally gone from your life.

This doesn't mean that the *stressors* are gone; lots of things will still happen around you, and some *to* you. What's different is *you*. It's how you react to what happens in your life. It's feeling calm instead of frazzled, angry, out of balance, and frustrated. This inner calmness and peace makes your day flow much better, even if the events are exactly the same. You'll feel better both while at work and at night when you're at home. You'll be much better able to enjoy time with your family, and they'll be able to enjoy time with you, too.

There are, of course, many other things that get better too, but eliminating stress is one of the most important, if not the most important (at least relating to today's society), benefit that comes from reaching a deeper spiritual perspective. Many positive things spring from there, and the effects of your peace and calmness ripple out to affect others in a widening circle. And this is from just *one* of the things that get better in your life and the lives of those around you. By itself, that benefit alone seems like a great reason to pursue a deeper spiritual understanding.

But naturally, the benefits go even deeper. As it turns out, having more and more people with a deep spiritual perspective is the best way to solve most, or all, of the problems in our society.

People who are spiritually open, spiritually awake, or spiritual masters voluntarily make positive choices and choose to do what's right. No government official needs to tell them what to do; no law needs to compel them. Their actions are already aimed at creating the highest good for all so no government involvement is needed for them to make this choice. The more people we have making choices that benefit everyone, the better everything will get.

This ultimately leads to a smaller government since people will already be living in accord with spiritual principles. A smaller government with less interference will lead to a stronger and more prosperous America. Even with a smaller government, Americans won't forget about the true disadvantaged. Those who genuinely need help will continue to get it from both our government and the local community around them. The community of spiritually aware people will recognize their need and take the actions necessary to help them – both through appropriate government programs, and, if needed, voluntarily – because it's the right thing to do. This is the America we can all live in; this America will be a true spiritual Republic.

In the next chapter I'll be describing a spiritual Republic. What I'm presenting in this chapter isn't a wistful dream. It can be very real, and we can begin to bring it into reality by the decisions we make today. Saying something is "just human nature" ignores our capacity to evolve and change our nature. In a sense, chalking things up as unchangeable due to human nature is a way to avoid taking responsibility for growth and change; to become more spiritual and better people than we are today. Let's see where the next step in our evolution can take us.

Part Four: The Spiritual Republic: Where we can be

In many ways, becoming a spiritual Republic is a logical step in America's development. As more people in the United States and around the world develop a stronger spiritual perspective and deeper spiritual understanding, our society will ultimately change to one more spiritual. America had a much stronger spiritual foundation at its beginning than it does now. It's clear we've gotten away from that foundation. It's time for us to return to our roots and move forward as an even greater nation.

We can develop a spiritual Republic from where we are today. The information in this section can help all of us and our heirs bring about much-needed positive change within the next few decades.

****

A spiritual Republic is a society that operates under spiritual and natural law. The individual is sovereign within a spiritual Republic, and the government exists to protect the rights of every individual. Every individual has the exact same rights as every other in a spiritual Republic. No "protected" classes need to exist because there are only individuals – all of whom have the exact same rights.

The real foundation of a spiritual Republic is its members having a deep spiritual awareness and understanding. That deep spiritual foundation leads to a society that values, and even requires, honesty, integrity, truthfulness, ethics, and respect. Also essential are doing the right thing and having fiscal responsibility. As a spiritual Republic, the United States will always live within its means and even generate surplus funds for unforeseen or emergency needs.

In the upcoming sections we'll look at a few things that have some overlap. We'll first take a look at some of the attributes of a spiritual Republic, then how those attributes can lead to a better society, and finally we'll cover some of the attributes of a person with a deeper spiritual understanding – a citizen of a spiritual Republic.

Here are some of the attributes of a spiritual Republic:

Most members of a spiritual Republic are spiritually open to at least some degree, and many are spiritually awake.

Right now, many people in this world are spiritually unaware (see the explanation on pg 72). A population at this level of spiritual awareness leads to what we have today – an unstable society with a serious lack of self-responsibility, a significant loss of respect, and severe fiscal mismanagement. This has led to many people in our society having an entitlement mentality – one in which "the government" is ultimately responsible for their well-being, instead of their being self-responsible. This obviously doesn't include everyone in society, but some people in society having an entitlement mentality negatively affects everyone in some way.

People immersed in the entitlement mentality can't reach their full growth and potential as a person. The productive members of society have a responsibility to support people who are functionally disabled. In today's welfare system, there are some people receiving benefits who aren't functionally disabled and who could, with a measure of self-respect (and possibly some education), support themselves. These extra people add more bureaucratic workload, and this means a larger government and greater costs to taxpayers.

Citizens of a spiritual Republic are kind, caring, courteous, respectful, and comfortable doing the right thing.

We'll go over more of these citizen attributes a bit later, but these five are definite cornerstones to the society we can have as a spiritual Republic. If you care to indulge in a bit of daydreaming, just imagine what a society would be like if these qualities were pervasive. What could a society of this type achieve? In all likelihood, many extraordinary things. Yes, we *can* have such a society here in America, and sooner than you may think.

There is little to no crime in a spiritual Republic.

When most members of a society are spiritually open or spiritually awake, there will naturally be very little crime. Crime is incompatible with genuine spiritual awareness, so the population will almost universally be voluntarily law-abiding citizens.

This means there will only be a small criminal element, if any, so our cities and towns will be much safer. This will in part be due to our citizens, being spiritually aware and self-responsible, taking an active role in ensuring the safety of their neighborhood and their families. With fewer crimes comes less economic cost, and this will add to our prosperity. Plus, as crime is substantially reduced or eliminated, the violence that accompanies crime will diminish as well. With citizens being spiritually aware, violence will diminish even further since disagreements will rarely, if ever, lead to physical violence.

There are no unnecessary wars.
A spiritual Republic will *always* protect its citizens and their way of life. Until the world has reached the point where no countries engage in war, the United States, even though it may be a spiritual Republic, could be attacked. The best protection against this is true military *might*. Those who would try to destroy our citizens, our country, and our way of life would be wise to tremble at the thought and seriously reconsider. That's because a true spiritual Republic will be powerful enough to eliminate any true threat – and will do so swiftly and decisively.

On the surface this may not seem to be a spiritual perspective, but it surely is. Our military will only be used for defense and never conquest. Defending our nation, citizens, and way of life is proper under the natural law of self-defense. It's proper under the spiritual principle of self-responsibility, in which we are fully responsible for our own well-being.

It's also important to recognize that the level of violence in any conflict is in the aggressor's hands. We won't fight unless we're defending, so any aggressor will bear sole responsibility for initiating the conflict. How far they're willing to go dictates how far we will have to go to stop them. Again, it's entirely in their hands. The best choice is obviously peace, and the world will experience greater peace as more countries see the benefits and become spiritual Republics.

There is no greed or jealousy.
Deep spiritual understanding results in a perspective that doesn't have room for greed. This perspective includes the truth that abundance is a natural spiritual state, and we only need to take actions that are for the highest good and in accord with spiritual

principles so we can tap into the natural abundance of this world. Without greed, most, or nearly all people will be very happy with having a comfortable life. Most of us won't feel a strong need to accumulate enormous amounts of wealth, although there is no spiritual reason you can't, if you choose – provided you accumulate your wealth honestly and ethically.

There will still be wealthy people, of course, and even more of them than there are now. That's because wealth will be seen as a tool to use for positive things, and to support our society and way of life. In a wealthy community, modest contributions from a fairly large number of families could go a long way toward helping those who genuinely need financial support and have no other options or recourse. In a way, it will be like going back to our past when neighbors would pitch in to help those in need.

There won't be any need to be jealous of neighbors and what they have. In a spiritual Republic, your rewards come from your choices and the products of your efforts. Every person in this Republic knows that any limits in their lives come from their choices. There will be no need to be jealous of anything that anyone else has since having what we want is really up to each of us and no one else.

Smoking and illegal drug use are eliminated by choice and gambling addiction is essentially eradicated.
Along with spiritual awareness comes an understanding that some of the choices we've made in the past have hurt our health. Pretty much all of us know that smoking leads to health risks and is a bad choice. We all know as well that using illegal drugs is simply foolish and very harmful.

In our spiritual Republic, the average citizen will be able to overcome virtually any addictions they may have, and very few, if any, younger members of the Republic will choose to smoke or use illegal drugs. Therefore, these behaviors will dwindle, fade, and die out over a relatively short period of time. Keep in mind that all this will come about by *choice*. It won't be from government regulation telling us we can't smoke; we simply won't want to. We'll eventually win the "war" on drugs by not taking them.

The same thing will happen with gambling addictions. People will no longer choose such destructive behavior and this, too, will fade. All of this may seem a bit pie-in-the-sky to some readers, and I don't mind telling you straight up that you're wrong. Human nature *can* change; we *can* grow to be better than we are. And we will do that by deepening our spiritual understanding and awareness. With that change, all these other changes become possible.

Clean energy and a clean environment are recognized as essential to long-term survival.
It should be plain to everyone reading this that we have damaged our home. We've polluted the planet, depleted some of its resources, and destroyed a great deal of life in the name of "progress" – simply due to ignorance and arrogance. That arrogance has no place in a spiritual Republic, so everyone in the Republic will want to do their part, in whatever way they can, to help heal and preserve our planet and not continue to ruin it.

It will be important to everyone in the Republic because all citizens will recognize the truth: that there will be generations after us, and these future generations need a home, too. More than a home – they need and deserve a *clean* home. Doing our best to resolve as many of these problems as we can is essential, and it's the spiritually right thing to do. It's wrong on many levels to burden future generations with a polluted home and a destroyed environment. While we may not be able to finish the job before we're gone (since it is an enormous task), we cannot have a clear conscience unless we have stopped making the problem worse and have at least started to fix this mess.

That means we absolutely need to spend time, money, and effort on creating clean, renewable forms of energy. This is at least as important as cleaning the environment since we won't gain much ground by our efforts until we have cleaner sources of renewable energy. It's time to start phasing out fossil fuels, regardless of how loudly oil and gas companies may protest.

Their profits are not nearly as important as our health is, and the health of our environment. The oil and gas companies would be wise to change their perception about their business. Here is a suggestion I'd like to make to them: Why not think of yourselves as *energy* companies, and lead America into the next phase of clean energy with your significant resources? It seems far better to do that, and to ensure your long-term viability as a business, than to put all your efforts into trying to squeeze out every last drop of oil and gas despite all the damage it's causing. Think about the future. Think about what you need to change so your company can move forward and be a thriving part of our spiritual Republic. If you don't, you will not be here in the future. The choice is yours.

Clean air and water, and healthful, unadulterated food are the norm.
The citizens of a spiritual Republic recognize that their personal health is important. Not only is it personally important, it's important to their family and to the society so they're healthy enough to make the greatest contribution they're able, while not hanging on to habits that make them sick and in need of expensive medical care.

With that level of priority given to health, the citizens will collectively choose to ensure that the air they breath, the water they drink, and the food they eat all work toward maintaining optimal health. This means their attention to the environment and commitment to clean energy will keep the air cleaner. The same will hold true for water. Once the society is dumping fewer pollutants into the water supply, it becomes much easier to make that water cleaner, safer, and more healthful to drink – and it will take less energy to do this.

There will be an enormous difference in the food supply of a spiritual Republic as compared to the highly processed and nutrient devoid packaged items that are currently passed off as food. Without greed, we'll be able to turn away from our focus on higher yield at less cost (regardless of the health effects) and return to natural foods that actually nourish our bodies. There will be less consumption of the pseudo foods that harm our bodies, such as modern genetically altered wheat and corn, sugar in its various forms, chemical sugar substitutes, and carbonated beverages.

Religious organizations and their political influences fade away, and are replaced by a deep understanding of spiritual principles.

While religious organizations do have some people who try to make a difference, they are too often managed and populated by people who lack true spiritual awareness and who are looking for personal power. Most of these people only give "lip service" to spiritual principles. Not surprisingly, this outer "apparent" spirituality is often a cover for negative actions and negative choices.

As spiritual people, we can organize without separating into groups with different names and different "angles" on religion and spirituality. By doing this, we can remove all of the dogmatic limitations that we currently have in our various religious organizations. By removing the dogma and differences, we'll be focusing on the true foundational principles of real spirituality. Over time, we'll be bound into a much stronger society since most people will share a common spiritual foundation. We can then gather as communities, further strengthening our local bonds and friendships.

This process will not put an end to religion. Instead, it opens up a deeper level of spiritual understanding to more people. There will be more unity in the message since the focus will be on the deep spiritual principles that are important to all of us as spiritually open and spiritually awake people. A more unified spiritual message will help our society fully embrace a spiritual foundation, and will help in forming and preserving a spiritual Republic.

A spiritual Republic has, and celebrates, cultural diversity without creating separate sub-cultures within its society.
This is more important than it may seem to be on the surface, and absolutely does NOT mean that people of different ethnic backgrounds will not be able to keep their cultural and ancestral beliefs. What it *does* mean is that every person in every cultural group is also an *American,* and an integrated part of American culture and society.

It's important to ensure that every citizen self-identifies as an American. This unity is important to the safety and security of our nation, and it's important to the uniqueness of the United States as a spiritual Republic. In this way, no sub-cultures can create separate bastions within the borders of our nation that could be comprised of people who are opposed to our way of life and want to harm our people and our society. While they're welcome to their personal beliefs, they're not welcome to stay if they enter our country under false pretenses to damage and subvert our way of life. We don't need them here if that's the way they feel. Naturally, we welcome anyone who is willing to embrace our ideals.

A better society with a spiritual Republic

Now that we've looked at some of the attributes of a spiritual Republic, let's see how our society could benefit from embracing these principles and using them as the foundation of what we can become.

The population of a spiritual Republic is either spiritually open, spiritually awake, or at some level of spiritual mastery.
We fundamentally change our consciousness for the better as we collectively deepen our spiritual perceptions and perspectives. With a strong spiritual foundation, our populace will be far less in the grip of negative emotions. Members will be calmer and more at peace, and almost invariably will choose to do what's right. With a deeper understanding of cause and effect, each person will be aware of how their actions affect others around them, and even what effects will ripple out from those actions.

This will absolutely lead to less need for government oversight in our daily affairs. People will be nearly self-governing because, in a very real sense, people's perspectives will be growing more divine. Even at the time of the Constitution's writing, people recognized that a truly spiritual perspective would result in proper government. James Madison, writing in Federalist Papers #51, put it this way:

> "If men were angels, no government would be necessary. If angels were to govern men, neither external nor internal controls on government would be necessary. In framing a government which is to be administered by men over men, the great difficulty lies in this: you must first enable the government to control the governed; and in the next place oblige it to control itself."

In a very real sense, developing a deep spiritual understanding very closely recreates the perspective of an angel inside a person here on

Earth. This is not merely theoretical, nor is it an unreachable state for all of us who are here right now on this planet. Each of us *can* genuinely reach a more divine perspective.

Here is the reason: it's clear that humanity evolves. Most of us evolve and become better people. Deep spiritual understanding and realization is a firm path to becoming much more enlightened than we are right now. That enlightened state is akin to "the mind of an angel." In time, this evolution is inevitable. We *will* evolve to be more like angels and believing it is possible is a necessary first step. Believing it's possible gives us a reason to work toward this goal now, and not wait for some future time when we finally believe we can indeed become more like angels – because we already have.

The individual is sovereign in a spiritual Republic.
What this means is simple: the *people,* and not the government, hold the real power. The government holds only what power is conveyed to it by the people, as specified in our Constitution. In a spiritual Republic, the governmental power is wielded by ethical representatives who act according to the will of the people.

This means that the government will no longer be able to run amok and act against the will of the people. Our current government has inappropriately seized powers away from the States and the people because these actions went unopposed. That will not happen in a spiritual Republic because the representatives will be driven by ethics instead of being driven by greed and power. If a representative does act against the will of the citizens, the citizens will correct the situation by taking appropriate action – most likely by removing and replacing the representative.

One of the government's primary roles is to preserve the rights and property of every individual.
No longer will our government chip away at our rights and liberties. Instead, the government of a spiritual Republic will champion those rights and fiercely protect them. To truly understand this, it's important to recognize that the government *is not the source of our rights.* Although we generally live by the whims of the government right now, that's only because it has usurped ownership of *our* rights. The Founders and Framers viewed our rights as God-given and an extension of Natural Law. In this

context, our rights are not the government's to grant; they're ours already, and *protecting* these rights is the government's responsibility.

Keep in mind that preserving our liberties does not give people in society the license to be out of control and run rampant, doing anything they feel like doing. The likelihood of this happening in a deeply spiritual society is very, very low. Each individual has the freedom to express their free will, but his actions must remain within those allowable by established laws and must not cause harm to others.

Smaller government with less regulation naturally evolves as most of the population makes ethical decisions by choice.
As spiritually open and spiritually awake people, the members of a spiritual Republic are self-guided to choose actions that are for the highest good. As such, the role of government will naturally shrink. After all, if most of the population is already, **by choice**, doing what is right, then there will be very little need for the government to compel anyone to do anything. Less government regulation will directly result in more prosperity for Americans – and it will be an *ethical* prosperity.

The government then takes on its proper roles: protecting citizens' rights, protecting the country from outside threats, and operating within the powers granted by Article 1, Section 8 of the Constitution, shown here:

> **"Section 8.** The Congress shall have Power To lay and collect Taxes, Duties, Imposts and Excises, to pay the Debts and provide for the common Defence and general Welfare of the United States; but all Duties, Imposts and Excises shall be uniform throughout the United States;
> To borrow Money on the credit of the United States;
> To regulate Commerce with foreign Nations, and among the several States, and with the Indian Tribes;
> To establish an uniform Rule of Naturalization, and uniform Laws on the subject of Bankruptcies throughout the United States;
> To coin Money, regulate the Value thereof, and of foreign Coin, and fix the Standard of Weights and Measures;

To provide for the Punishment of counterfeiting the Securities and current Coin of the United States;

To establish Post Offices and post Roads;

To promote the Progress of Science and useful Arts, by securing for limited Times to Authors and Inventors the exclusive Right to their respective Writings and Discoveries;

To constitute Tribunals inferior to the Supreme Court;

To define and punish Piracies and Felonies committed on the high Seas, and Offenses against the Law of Nations;

To declare War, grant Letters of Marque and Reprisal, and make Rules concerning Captures on Land and Water;

To raise and support Armies, but no Appropriation of Money to that Use shall be for a longer Term than two Years;

To provide and maintain a Navy;

To make Rules for the Government and Regulation of the land and naval Forces;

To provide for calling forth the Militia to execute the Laws of the Union, suppress Insurrections and repel Invasions;

To provide for organizing, arming, and disciplining, the Militia, and for governing such Part of them as may be employed in the Service of the United States, reserving to the States respectively, the Appointment of the Officers, and the Authority of training the Militia according to the discipline prescribed by Congress;

To exercise exclusive Legislation in all Cases whatsoever, over such District (not exceeding ten Miles square) as may, by Cession of particular States, and the Acceptance of Congress, become the Seat of the Government of the United States, and to exercise like Authority over all Places purchased by the Consent of the Legislature of the State in which the Same shall be, for the Erection of Forts, Magazines, Arsenals, dock-Yards, and other needful Buildings; — And

To make all Laws which shall be necessary and proper for carrying into Execution the foregoing Powers, and all other Powers vested by this Constitution in the Government of the United States, or in any Department or Officer thereof."

Businesses are free from greed and fundamentally capable of self-regulating.

Since a deepening spiritual awareness brings with it a voluntary willingness and desire to do what's right, business owners and managers will naturally begin operating this way. Business will be transacted with a deep sense of integrity and personal responsibility. This personal feeling of responsibility will spread to include satisfying customers, ensuring a safe, high-quality product, and ensuring that the business does no significant damage to the environment.

When businesses are voluntarily choosing to operate ethically, voluntarily embracing conservation and maintaining the environment, and ensuring the quality and safety of their products, there will no longer be any need to legislatively compel them to do these things. This means that the "alphabet soup" of government agencies will be pared down to only those which are genuinely necessary.

Ethically operating a business also includes appropriately compensating employees; greater skills on the part of employees lead to greater pay. Business profits will be factored into business operations, but there will be no need to drive those profits to levels of excess by cutting corners and cheating employees and consumers. The net effect of this will be to substantially reduce poverty and raise the average standard of living. It will all be done without a single government regulation.

People outgrow greed and all the negative things caused by it.
Greed is incredibly destructive. It affects every level of society so it's very pervasive. Greed causes a large number of negative behaviors, including armed conflicts, robberies, manipulating others, cheating other people, deceit, taking advantage of others, emotional injuries, and many other negative things. In fact, overcoming greed will probably do more good for society than overcoming almost any other obstacle.

Once we, as a society, overcome greed, other changes will come along in the process. Some people who are currently making negative choices based on greed will change, since they'll come to genuinely understand that theft and robbery are wrong. Once they do this, they'll change their choices and begin to earn the money they need to live by legitimate means. At the corporate level, not operating businesses to generate excessive profits will help reduce prices and the cost of living. Employees will likely earn more and this will help reduce poverty. In addition, most businesses are likely to hire at least some additional employees if their current employees are substantially overworked. A side effect of this will be reduced employee stress in most places of business, which will obviously have broad-range positive effects.

These outcomes probably seem really far-fetched to some readers. If that's you, at least take a moment to imagine life without greed and see what you come up with. Whatever it is, it's likely to be a step in the right direction.

Society is safer and more secure.
The citizens of a spiritual Republic, being more spiritually aware, will naturally make more positive choices. This is because the average level of wisdom will be greater than that of our current society. Because of this, most, or nearly all, will naturally and voluntarily stop negative behaviors such as smoking, using illegal drugs, and drunk driving.

Violent crime will be exceedingly rare, as will personal violence between individuals. This all comes about with a deeper spiritual understanding, which leads to a better understanding of cause and effect. A better understanding of cause and effect leads to making choices that will have less negative effects. This brings about the highest good possible, because we learn that the consequences of our actions often have *other* consequences, and these consequences can ripple out and continue to affect other people. People begin to understand the deeper ramifications of what they do, and that makes it even more important to make the best choices possible.

Having a deep spiritual understanding makes it easier to make right choices. All the negative things in our society are a result of making one or more negative choices. Making a positive choice instead of a negative choice changes the outcome of any situation. Anyone can select a positive choice over a negative choice at any time and with every choice. All of us can do this *right now*. There is no need to wait until you feel you have reached a deep level of spiritual understanding to begin to make better choices. You can start today because each ethical and positive choice made helps to transform society for the better.

People have a deep understanding of personal responsibility and community responsibility.

An important part of having a spiritual perspective is the idea of personal responsibility. Someone who doesn't understand the true nature of personal responsibility is constantly blaming someone else for the results of their actions. You'll often hear exclamations similar to "It's not my fault!" or other statements that duck responsibility and put the blame on someone else.

Someone who lacks a sense of personal responsibility doesn't have the point of view needed to develop a sense of community responsibility, either. They don't generally understand the broader consequences of their actions, so they're unable to see that their actions are sometimes at the root of things that happen around them.

On the other hand, having a real spiritual perspective brings a sense of personal and community responsibility. A person who is spiritually open or awake realizes that their actions have consequences beyond the obvious. Most of their choices will be given deeper consideration, and will be more carefully thought out than the choices made by people without a spiritual perspective. As a result, it becomes easier to make more positive choices and to take responsibility for the outcome of those choices.

This sense of personal responsibility often extends to other people because a spiritual person thinks about how their actions will affect people around them. Even though everyone around them is responsible for the effects of their own actions, a spiritual person, without fail, will take responsibility for their own actions and correct any problems that arise as a result of their choices. This way no one else has to fix any problems they've caused by their actions. In other words, a spiritual person fixes their own mistakes.

This point of view extends to include a sense of personal responsibility for the community as well. This means that a person with a deeply spiritual perspective will care about the well-being of the people around them and the area around them. People with a spiritual perspective help others in their community simply because it's right to do so; they don't need any other reason. In this way, people help others because they *choose* to, and the people providing the help know their aid went where they intended and that it was used properly. There is no longer personal involvement or personal choice when the government usurps this sense of personal responsibility; when all aid comes from the government, resources that could have directly helped others are spent on bureaucracy and the aid is sometimes misused.

Lastly, having a large number of people taking personal responsibility for their lives and the community effectively reduces or even eliminates the society-destroying effects of entitlement thinking. Having a large number of people thinking that society simply "owes" them, and who stay in entitlement programs without a real medical reason, weakens our society by promoting a non-productive lifestyle that sometimes leads to various forms of crime. A deep sense of personal responsibility eliminates this problem.

Roadways are safer.
As more people become spiritually open and spiritually awake, the members of our society will become more calm, centered, and peaceful. Calmer people will generally be less "in a hurry," and road rage will essentially disappear. In addition, people will voluntarily choose to limit numerous risky behaviors, such as: speeding, not signaling, phoning/texting while driving, and erratic driving.

As a result, people will place greater importance on paying attention while driving and on driving safely. The net result will be far fewer accidents. This will obviously save lives, but it will also save on insurance costs and auto repair expenses.

Emotions and ego are no longer the driving force behind our society.
There will be a momentous change in our society when this happens. Let's stop for a moment to consider how much our lives are currently influenced by our emotions and ego. To recap: The ego is our personal sense of self, and its proper function is to act as a messenger between the soul and the physical body. When the veil is in place, the ego has lost contact with the soul and is essentially on its own, filling a role it was not designed for and doesn't perform well.

We experience a great deal of strife and stress when our emotions and ego run our lives. The world appears chaotic and like a very negative place. We respond by using our negative emotions as protection. When we respond this way, we feel and display emotions such as fear, anger, hurt feelings, greed, despondency, despair, hopelessness, and many others. We also feel and express positive emotions, but those often come from events in our lives that cheer us up. This means they tend to be transitory, which is unfortunate. Our positive emotions come to the front and become our "default" emotions when we genuinely reach a deep spiritual perspective.

We find that we feel more emotionally balanced as our spiritual perspective deepens and our understanding grows. We feel more joy; our emotions are more tempered and we're more accepting of others exactly as they are. We also find that our drive for self-improvement begins to dominate our lives. This comes from having our soul in control of our daily life, instead of our ego having control. In this state, the ego is subordinate to the soul and fulfilling its proper function. As such, the rampant, mainly negative, emotions of the ego do not hold sway over us so our behavior is stable and positive rather than erratic and negative. All of this ultimately leads to a more stable, prosperous, and peaceful society in which every individual is offered the best opportunity to reach their full potential.

Interactions and agreements are equitable and agreeable to all parties.
By growing into a true spiritual Republic, members of our society will naturally outgrow most negative emotions. The negative emotion that most affects business is greed. We've already touched on the benefits of outgrowing greed, but we're going to look at this specific context, agreements (or contracts) and business interactions, a bit closer.

There is no doubt that many people in business today operate fair and honest businesses, but there are others who don't. In the end, we'll see that most, or nearly all, businesses in a spiritual Republic will, *by choice*, be ethical, honest businesses operating with fairness and integrity.

There are several basic types of business interactions. The most significant of these are company/customer, company/vendor, and company/employee. The businesses that are out to maximize profits often seek to charge the customer as much as possible, pay their vendors and employees as little as possible, and overwork their employees. This business is obviously operating under negative conditions.

Employees are generally unhappy and dissatisfied in businesses like this, vendor relations are often strained, and the customer is frequently also dissatisfied. It should be obvious that this is a stressful way to run a business. Employee turnover is likely to be high, and the business probably relies heavily on their marketing for a constant influx of new customers – or a "captive" market for repeat customers. Fortunately, there is a much better way to conduct business.

A business operated by people who are spiritually open and who understand cause and effect will focus their efforts on producing a high-quality product or service that meets or exceeds what their customer pays for. They work to *over-deliver*, at least a bit, to ensure their customer gets a great value. Most customers, of course, notice this and reward the business with repeat business.

A business operated under spiritual principles has a much better relationship with their vendors as well. While the business operators know they need a profit to stay in business, they also recognize that their vendor needs to stay in business too. This protects their business and their vendor's business, and their vendors surely recognize and appreciate it. When temporary supply issues or other problems arise, they all work together to find the best solution for the problem.

The relationship with the business's employees is far better as well, when compared to a negatively-operated business. The business owners or managers recognize the vital contribution their employees make, and will not treat them as expendable. Turnover and training costs are much lower with genuinely happy employees because they are far more loyal and tend to have more time on the job. Employees tend to become more skilled and the customers notice this difference, too. Plus, the employees will be appropriately paid, rather than mistreated and shorted raises so the management can get their annual pay raise or profit sharing bonus.

All of this leads to a more stable and consistently profitable business. There will be less stress for everyone, and output quality will be both greater and effectively self-policed. Productivity and reputation for quality both grow dramatically when most businesses are operating at this level across our nation.

Now let's take a brief look at the idea of agreements being equitable and agreeable to all parties.

Agreement in business typically means *contract*. A lot of litigation occurs each year from various businesses, for various reasons, breaking their agreements. Some of these breaches are legitimate and unavoidable. Some happen because the business finds that fulfilling their agreement is so unfavorable that risking litigation seems like a viable alternative. Business in a spiritual Republic will significantly change a great deal of the latter type.

In a spiritual Republic, business people know that unpredictable events happen. Catastrophes strike, often without warning. When this happens, both parties affected by the catastrophe will work together to resolve the problem. This certainly happens in business today, but more business owners and managers opt for litigation in resolving these difficulties than is really necessary. In a spiritual Republic, litigation will be a rare event after a catastrophe.

Unfavorable agreements will also be few and far between. Businesses in a spiritual Republic will naturally want favorable terms for their business, but will not push to stack the deck entirely in their favor, and will not accept the terms of any agreement that obviously hurts the other party in the agreement, because it is spiritually wrong to do so. The people in the other business are due appropriate compensation for their efforts, and the business needs a profit to continue operating. Arranging agreements in this way is good for all the businesses involved, and leads to all parties in the agreement feeling satisfied with the arrangement and feeling that their interests are protected.

104

It's highly likely that having businesses take this approach will substantially reduce litigation, and we all know litigation bears a high cost that negatively affects business owners, employees, and their customers. The time and cost of litigation decreases productivity while increasing expenses. While litigation will be necessary at times, in a spiritual Republic it will be used far less than it is today.

We focus on long-term and sustainable solutions for existing problems, rather than looking for a quick fix or promoting special interests.
One of the hallmarks of a spiritual Republic is that the citizens and government alike will work out solutions to problems that are environmentally responsible, fiscally responsible, and have the most positive outcome for the greatest number of citizens – not the government or large corporations.

Many choices made by businesses and our government, past and present, fail to take the long-term effects of their actions into account when making decisions. As a result, we currently have a system that protects profit at the expense of the environment, ahead of employees' well-being, and ahead of providing value to customers. Many government regulations tend to follow the money. Since many business owners and managers focus on lowest cost and highest profit, they ignore virtually all of the long-term effects of their choices. This often negatively impacts health in entire neighborhoods, and can lead to releasing poisons into our air, water, and ground.

These negative effects will rarely happen in a spiritual Republic. Instead, businesses will operate ethically and with concern for the environment and people. All of the environmental and health risks, both immediate and long-term, will be factors in making decisions. We will collectively choose cleaner alternatives so we will be adding less pollution to our planet. Less pollution will lead to a cleaner environment, and a cleaner environment naturally leads to better health and a better quality of life for everyone.

It's important to remember that *we can do this*. It's a matter of putting the environment and people's health ahead of profit. We can start this *today*. Greater spiritual awareness leads to more responsible choices and we can make a decision to be more responsible right now. There is no need to wait for a later time. Every step we take counts, and letting problems grow means we and our progeny have to work harder to solve them – or worse, we can ignore them and wait for them to be too big to solve. If that happens, we will have doomed ourselves and much of the life on Earth.

Society will focus on developing the cleanest and safest sustainable energy and not on wringing out every last drop of profit regardless of the environmental cost.
We naturally develop a deeper understanding of the effects of our actions as our spiritual awareness grows. We already know our current ways of producing and using energy are harming us and our planet. While it's true we're currently working on other options, those other options are unfolding slowly so the big oil companies can drain out every last drop of profit.

In a spiritual Republic, clean energy will be more important than profit. More time, effort, and money will be spent on developing clean and renewable energy sources, and technologically adapting those sources to our way of life. We have the capacity to do this right now, but too few research funds are available to properly advance new energy technologies. A spiritual perspective will help our society develop a longer-term view than we have right now. When we add in the greater prosperity possible in a spiritual Republic, it becomes easier to see how we will eventually develop the resources to make clean, renewable energy the energy backbone of our society.

The citizens of a spiritual Republic recognize the importance of healthful food and clean water.
It seems apparent that we're on the wrong track when it comes to our food and health. Poor food choices still predominate in our society despite all the recommendations out there. We place more emphasis on convenience than what is healthful or hurtful to our bodies. Health care does pick up some slack, but our current system focuses more on curing symptoms rather than eliminating the behaviors and choices that are causing many of our health problems. Getting and remaining healthy should be a priority for everyone.

Obesity, heart disease, and cancer keep growing epidemically. It should be obvious to anyone that our current health recommendations and food processing are leading us down a path of destruction. In this situation, as in others, it's time to get back to basics and stop putting so much emphasis on convenience. If you don't think we're heading in the wrong direction, then get out some old family photo albums. Take a look at your family pictures from 50 or 60 years ago. Then take a look at your latest family photos.

You won't be able to deny that we are much fatter and generally less healthy than our ancestors. Technology in our health care system has certainly improved. Imagine applying those improvements to a healthier population. Not only would costs go down, but just imagine how much longer we'll be able to live, and how much of a better lifestyle we'll be able to enjoy as fit, healthy people.

The changes we need to make start at home. We need to break away from processed foods, GMO foods, excess sugar, and even carbonated beverages. Let's have more families with home gardens, and let's eat more local produce. People will be healthier and food costs will go down if more families plant gardens. It's also an opportunity to teach our children valuable lessons about a sustainable way of life. It's easy to make more of your land productive by planting a garden and fruit and nut trees. For families who want to take the extra steps, learning about *permaculture* can help you transform your home site from a long list of chores into a life-sustaining space.

Over the long term, these changes will improve commercial food production as well. More emphasis will be placed on local farms, and farmer's markets will become even more prevalent than they are now. In this way, our food will be shipped far shorter distances, rather than the thousands of miles that some of our food has to travel now. Lower transportation costs should lead to lower final cost – not to mention the reduced gallons of gasoline and diesel fuel burned, and the pollution this generates.

Over time, commercial food growers will begin to integrate permaculture ideas to naturally increase yields and use fewer chemicals. Genetically modifying foods will also be reduced and eventually eliminated. It should be reasonably clear that genetically altering foods should be left to the process that evolved in nature and not be done by humans just because we can – with the potential for many unintended side-effects.

Large, chemically-based farms will become outmoded, because people will no longer accept genetically-altered, herbicide- and pesticide-laden foods that are most likely harmful to their health. Over time, these huge tracts of land will be cleansed and parceled out into a greater number of smaller scale organic farms. Food supplies will be more localized, cleaner, and much more nutritious.

Another benefit of healthier food choices is this: medical costs will naturally decrease as people get healthier and get fewer major illnesses, including cancer. Here is a thought regarding cancer: right now we're focused on *curing* cancer. How about we focus on *not causing it* instead? What we are currently doing to our environment and food are prime suspects in the explosion in cancer rates. Healthful living and fewer illnesses are two of the most important things that will happen as the United States develops into a spiritual Republic.

****

At this point, I want to reiterate a critical point: all the benefits of our society becoming a spiritual Republic hinge on its citizens becoming more spiritually aware. True spiritual awareness is the heart of a spiritual Republic. Since this shift is vital to the United States becoming a spiritual Republic, let's take a brief look at some of the attributes we'll find in citizens who are spiritually open or spiritually awake.

Attributes of citizens in a spiritual Republic

After reading this section, you will very likely see that having more members of society at this level of awareness, or greater, will clearly lead to a better society. That's why it's vital that each of us make this choice and pursue true spiritual growth – and help everyone around us (at least those who are willing) do the same.

A citizen of a spiritual Republic is self-responsible.

Someone who is spiritually aware takes responsibility for their own actions, and takes the actions needed to make things right or to bring things into balance. They'll take charge of correcting their mistakes and the problems brought about by those mistakes. A spiritually awake person will not look to others to provide solutions to their problems.

A person who is spiritually awake recognizes and understands *cause* **and** *effect.*
It's important to recognize that actions have consequences. There is nothing that we do that doesn't affect someone else, at least in some way. In most cases, although not all, negative actions lead to negative consequences, and positive actions lead to positive consequences. Therefore, choosing our actions carefully and understanding the repercussions of those actions helps each of us make positive choices instead of negative choices, which leads to more positive effects. In other words, doing the right thing most often leads to good things happening.

Another faculty that people with a spiritual perspective often develop is the ability to understand the deeper effects of their actions. They begin to understand that their actions have consequences, *and those consequences have consequences too.* Understanding the deeper consequences helps to ensure that our actions will have both immediate and long-term positive outcomes. Ensuring positive deeper outcomes in a sense amplifies the positive effects of making good choices.

Having a deep spiritual understanding also helps when confronted with difficult choices, since this understanding provides a solid framework that focuses on actions that produce the *highest* good for everyone. As a side note, I'd like to mention that tearing down some people to give a boost to others is NOT a spiritually right action or choice. In a spiritual society, those who need the boost will get it – *without* tearing down or harming anyone else in the process.

A spiritually open person treats other people with courtesy and respect.
Being spiritually open includes the understanding that the person we see is not the *whole* person – they have a deeper part (their "soul"), and that deeper part is the greater and more important part of them. Their soul is also the part of the other person that *we* are most like. There may be many differences in the physical world, but

those differences disappear at the level of the soul, and we are much more alike as soul than different.

With this perspective, it's easier to respect the *soul* of the person even if the person is doing things we, as a person, don't like or that we disagree with. With this basis, it becomes easier to act respectfully toward others and to treat them with courtesy. People generally respond better to respect and courtesy than they do to disrespect and discourtesy. Treating others with respect acknowledges their value and reduces the stress in both people's lives. It's a more positive way to live, and treating others respectfully will be an important part of life in a spiritual Republic.

Treating others with respect goes hand-in-hand with self-respect, and self-respect is a crucial part of spiritual growth. In fact, without self-respect, the best anyone can hope for is the *appearance* of spiritual growth. People in this situation often have a mental understanding of spiritual principles, but have not yet experienced the shift from mental understanding to genuine spiritual realization. This means that there are outward actions and words that mimic spiritual growth, but there is little or no internal sense of value and self-worth. True spiritual realization brings with it the knowledge that all life, including our own, is of real, inestimable value.

A spiritually aware person treats their personal possessions, other's possessions, and common areas with respect.
This is really an extension of the previous statement. An internal feeling of self-worth and self-respect not only leads to treating others with respect, it also includes treating our possessions, other's possessions, and common areas with respect as well. This means using care with our personal possessions and anything we use that belongs to someone else. It also includes safe and proper use of common areas, such as streets, sidewalks, and public buildings. The term "proper use" *excludes* things like stealing, defacing property, littering, or deliberately damaging property.

As you can see, the spiritual basis for respect and self-respect carries over into all aspects of our lives. The net effect of this perspective is ultimately a more polite and courteous society than what we currently have.

A deep spiritual understanding leads to being compassionate.
A person who is spiritually open knows that adverse circumstances beyond someone's control can happen to anyone at any time. They also know that our choices, despite how carefully we may make them, can still have negative consequences that may affect us and others. A person with a deep spiritual understanding will be willing to help someone else in any way possible, especially if the other person is taking responsibility for their actions and trying to make things right.

This willingness to help comes from understanding that any of us can encounter difficulties beyond our ability to handle on our own. There are times we all need other people to help us. A part of having a spiritual perspective is being willing to provide help when it's needed, and to ask for help when we find ourselves in need.

A spiritual perspective includes a high degree of honesty and integrity.
Honesty is essential to spirituality. Our soul recognizes only the truth; it's our ego that accepts and sometimes propagates lies. When we lie, our ego is in control of our lives and our soul isn't. We cannot have a truly spiritual perspective if our ego is in control. We can reach a mental understanding of spiritual principles with the ego in control, and that is an essential beginning step in our development. However, it's vital to take the next step – transitioning from mental understanding to spiritual realization – and this step can only be taken when your ego loosens its grip and your soul is ready to take control. This is what I call being spiritually *awake*.

Once we are spiritually awake, our soul is in control of our lives and actions. The soul does not lie, cheat, manipulate, choose to steal, choose to use illegal drugs, and will not choose to drive while drunk. The soul also recognizes the negative effects that come with gambling to the point of financial harm, along with the negative effects of other addictions, and refuses to participate in them.

This benefits society in many ways. Having more people in our society who are spiritually awake leads to a much higher degree of truthfulness in our population. Facing things truthfully generates far less strife and pain than lying does. Being truthful also leads to

111

greater cooperation in resolving problems. Having integrity means your actions match your words. When you wrap all these factors together, a high level of honesty and integrity in its citizens results in a society that is far less adversarial than the society we have today.

A citizen of a spiritual Republic uses a high degree of ethics at work, in business, and in their personal lives.
Ethics are just as important to a spiritually aware person as are honesty and integrity. With solid ethics in place, citizens in a spiritual Republic will regularly seek balanced and equitable outcomes to each transaction or situation. They'll actively seek out solutions that provide the most positive outcomes for the most people involved. They won't look out solely for their own interests, and won't agree to an outcome that takes advantage of someone else.

This already occurs to some degree in business today. But we can do better, and it's not unrealistic to anticipate that nearly 100% of business and personal transactions can conclude with everyone a "winner."

A person with a deep spiritual perspective is compelled to do what s/he feels is right and cannot be compelled to do what s/he feels is wrong.
This is a natural outgrowth of honesty, integrity, and ethics. A spiritually aware person would not deliberately choose to do something they know is wrong because doing so violates their sense of honesty, integrity, and ethics. A spiritually aware person will rarely, if ever, deliberately choose to do something hurtful to others. Mistakes can still be made; no one can be 100% right all the time. The difference is that the spiritually aware person felt that the actions which led to the mistake were the *right* choice at the time.

Similarly, this perspective would make it difficult indeed to try and talk someone into doing something wrong and compromising their integrity and ethics. People with a deep spiritual awareness place a tremendous value on their integrity. It's simply not for sale, and no material or status reward will sway them. This would be a highly desirable faculty in, for example, our elected representatives.

A spiritually open person recognizes that "feeling offended" is personal choice.
Someone with a spiritual point of view knows that every person's perspective reflects where they are spiritually. Because of this, they know that what a person finds offensive is a personal choice, and isn't the right point of view for *everyone*. They recognize that each person has a right to their personal perspectives and opinions. Because of this, people who are spiritually aware do not try to force others to think or feel the same way they do, believing it's the only "right" way to think or feel. In fact, spiritual people often choose to never *be* offended.

With a deeply spiritual perspective, individual rights are seen as the only true rights.
The simple fact is that every individual in society, regardless of wealth or status, has the same rights as every other individual in a spiritual Republic. This should be true in any and every society. Every single one of us is a soul in a physical body, and every soul is birthed from and connected to God. Is any one, single soul, as an aspect of God, more valuable than any other? The obvious answer is no, since any and every aspect of God has illimitable spiritual value, and that illimitable value is the *same* value for every soul. Think of it: every person you see has a spiritual value without limit.

From this perspective, it's easy to see that everyone, regardless of their station in life, deserves to be treated with honor and respect. People sometimes do things we don't like, but their choices and actions don't affect their value as a soul. It remains without limit.

Since all people and their souls have the same limitless spiritual value, it's easy to see that individual rights in our society should all be the same. With every individual having the same protected rights, there is no need for any "protected classes." That type of thinking is outmoded and limited, and ultimately hurts society by perpetuating differences where they don't exist. There was a time that having protected classes may have served a specific purpose, but that purpose, and the need for it, will not exist in a spiritual Republic. In a spiritual Republic, all citizens share the same rights and same access to opportunity. What they make of that opportunity is up to them and no one else. This is the *true* meaning of equality.

A spiritual citizen recognizes that society has rules to protect the safety, health and well-being of its members, and voluntarily follows these rules.

Rules make society possible. Without them, there can be no order and cooperation, little accumulated knowledge, and no societal advancement. Citizens with a spiritual perspective know how vital rules are to a society, and they choose to voluntarily follow society's rules. They may not agree with them all, but they know rules serve a critical purpose and that following them is far more important than their agreement or disagreement.

It's important to note that spiritual citizens, in choosing to follow rules (even rules they don't agree with), do so peacefully and without angst. If there is a difference between their perspective and society's rules, they don't let that difference create negative emotions inside them – negative emotions that could brew and lead to internal pressure, anger, and eventually breaking those rules.

Spiritual citizens see liberty as critical to the existence of a spiritual Republic.

Tyranny is directly opposed to a true spiritual perspective. Someone with spiritual awareness recognizes the sovereignty of each individual. Oppressing others and stripping them of their natural rights is a violation of spiritual law. Therefore, people with a spiritual perspective know that liberty is a natural law that goes hand-in-hand with self-responsibility.

Having both liberty and self-responsibility provides the best conditions for personal and spiritual growth, and also for developing a lasting, prosperous, and stable society. All citizens are encouraged to be the best person they can be. A society based on growth and self-improvement leads to far more advancement than a society designed to stifle all liberties. Such a society can only be stagnant and will ultimately fail. Tyranny can create some form of a society, but only liberty can lead to a *great* society.

Spiritual citizens do not tolerate crime and deliberate negative actions.

Breaking the law comes with consequences. And it's spiritually and morally correct for the person who broke the law to be the person who is punished. No innocent person should be punished for someone else's crime. This means that everyone is held accountable for their actions and has to bear responsibility for serving appropriate jail time, making restitution, and taking any other actions necessary to make up for what they did.

While it's probable that jails will still exist in a spiritual Republic, more criminals will be held directly accountable for repairing the damage they've done. There will certainly be some security issues to work out, but since there will be fewer crimes overall this should not present a real barrier. In addition, most people, when directly confronted with the consequences of their actions – and being responsible for correcting or repairing them – will have a much more personal reaction to the result of their crime. In many cases, this should lead to greater remorse and better choices in the future.

A person with a spiritual perspective promotes peace, but understands that others may do things that leave no alternative but to use violence against the perpetrator for self-protection, or to protect others and the Republic.
A citizen of a spiritual Republic would never choose to perpetrate violence against anyone else. However, the actions of another person may put them in a position of needing to respond with violence. The right of self-defense is a natural law, and natural laws are Universal Spiritual Laws.

Criminals make a conscious choice when they victimize someone else. The responsibility for what happens next falls entirely on the criminal, regardless of the outcome. A spiritual person placed in this situation has the same right as anyone else: to protect their person from bodily harm, to protect their life, or to protect someone else from bodily harm or loss of life. Acting according to that right can lead to harm or even death coming to the perpetrator. Since the situation only existed because of the perpetrator's actions, the spiritual person who uses violence against a criminal to stop the criminal's actions has no guilt or responsibility in the situation – as long as their actions stop once the threat has been neutralized.

Citizens in a spiritual Republic respect other cultures, but they know it is important to maintain and grow <u>American</u> culture.
Being a citizen of a spiritual Republic and sharing the rights of that Republic means accepting the responsibility that comes with being a

citizen. Part of that responsibility is protecting the Republic. A cohesive culture of Americans who want to be a part of our Republic and who want to protect the ideals of that Republic presents a strong, unified front for any groups that seek to destroy our Republic and way of life by infiltrating our society.

Until enough countries understand the benefits to their citizens of becoming a spiritual Republic, some of the other societies on Earth will set out to destroy us and our way of life, just as it is in the world today. All citizens need to be aware of this, and need to have a willingness to defend and protect our way of life. Every person has the right to honor their ancestors and their beliefs; what we need to watch for are groups of people separating from our society within our cities, using other laws, and creating an essentially independent society within ours.

People choosing to do this are choosing to live at odds with the principles of our spiritual Republic, and that choice will not be welcome or tolerated in our Republic. Honoring an ancestral culture *is* welcome, provided the group also remains a part of American society and culture.

Spiritual citizens understand that a spiritual Republic can and will serve as an example to other cultures.
In many cases, citizens of other nations will see the benefits that come from having a spiritual Republic as a form of government, and many will want those benefits for themselves. This will be a positive turn of events; as more nations aspire to and ultimately reach this form of government, the world will become far less violent and better able to assure global prosperity.

Citizens of a spiritual Republic know they need to remain vigilant and to keep the Republic strong, because there will be threats from other nations who have tyrannical regimes and who see our spiritual Republic as a threat to their way of life. Naturally, that is only their perception since one of the most basic tenets of a spiritual Republic is liberty – and that includes liberty for other people to live as they choose. Because of this, it's important that the Republic be powerful enough to prevail against those who would seek to attack it and attempt to tear it down.

Citizens of a spiritual Republic are willing to act in any capacity they need to and are able to, in order to support and maintain the society of the spiritual Republic.
This means that qualified citizens will often choose to serve the Republic in whatever way they can. Many will put aside their personal discomfort and fill roles they're qualified for but not eagerly seeking in order to help other citizens and to support the Republic. Their choices will be based on what the Republic needs, and not based on the citizen's preferences or comfort zone.

In some cases this will lead to citizens taking on roles they wouldn't prefer to have, but that they know they can perform well. People will begin running for public offices based on capability and not to seek power and influence. This will lead to greater overall capability in our public officials and far less corruption since greed and power will not be motivating factors. We know this is already true to some degree with some of our elected officials; obviously, not all are corrupt and motivated by greed and power. But some are. These corrupt politicians can be replaced by capable people motivated by enriching the Republic and its citizens. When this happens, our society will indeed take a truly positive turn.

Citizens of a spiritual Republic recognize the importance of a strong community and how important it is that the community members support and help each other.
Our immediate community is an important resource and is an essential part of our long-term well-being. It's important that community members support each other and not depend on others outside the community – especially a bloated, slow-operating federal government – for support during "normal" times and even most emergencies or disasters. Federal government help takes time to arrive, if it arrives at all. In a crisis, the community members may have only each other to rely on as resources.

Community members supporting each other in the normal course of day to day activity helps enormously when emergencies and disasters strike. Different community members have different resources and capabilities, but everyone has *something* to contribute. The community is always stronger when the people in that community stick together. This can be done in any size community and even in a large city, where your "community" may be an apartment building, or even a specific floor of that building. It begins with knowing your neighbors and learning which neighbors you can trust and depend on. Naturally, this will all become easier and more effective as greater numbers of our population grow into a deeper spiritual perspective.

A spiritually aware person recognizes that each community, and each person in it, is responsible for being a steward for their land and resources, and for maintaining a healthy local environment.
It seems obvious that future generations will need this planet too. It's irresponsible to ruin resources that will be needed by future generations. It's also greedy and short-sighted. People who are spiritually aware take proper care of the existing natural resources in order to ensure there are sufficient resources for future generations. Most people would agree that we are responsible for ensuring the land and environment are in good health and able to sustain our heirs in a clean and decent lifestyle.

Since we largely haven't done this, and since the movement to clean up our mess and develop cleaner energy is comparatively new, we need to put extra effort into both developing clean resources and cleaning up our mess. It's simply spiritually wrong to expect a number of future generations to suffer with our short-sightedness and to have to clean up the mess *we* made. We need to take responsibility for this and put more attention on the pollution we're creating so we can stop making things worse and start making them better.

Maintaining a clean local environment simply makes sense. After all, each of us has to live in our neighborhood, unless we plan to drain all the good resources, destroy the environment and then move on. I don't think this describes most Americans, and it certainly doesn't describe anyone who is spiritually open. Keeping our land and water clean is something every one of us can help with right now to ensure usable and renewable resources for future generations.

A spiritually open citizen recognizes the importance of the Earth's environment, in addition to the local environment.
We are slowly working toward cleaner and renewable energy resources, and working toward generating less pollution. However,

we need to put more emphasis, time, and money into these efforts. We must support and seek out safe and commercially viable forms of renewable and clean energy, and expand our efforts through safe, honest innovation to provide for our future energy needs.

At least for now, Earth is the only home we all have. We need its resources and we need to work within the environmental capabilities of the Earth, along with its natural cleansing processes, to maintain it as a viable home for our species. We have no way of knowing if we'll eventually be able to colonize worlds outside of our solar system. We may have alternatives in the future if we can. If it turns out it's extremely difficult to leave our solar system due to technological limits and the laws of physics, then we have no fallback plan at all. Our choice could ultimately be to either live in harmony with the Earth or to perish.

Many citizens are coming to realize that we need to take substantial action to protect our future. Many people are starting now, beginning with their personal space and local community. Small positive changes over a wide area eventually add together into larger and larger swaths of healthy land and water. In time, these swaths accumulate and will eventually bring the way we live into harmony and balance with the Earth.

Our need to conserve and preserve includes *all* resources: water, energy, air, food, land, minerals, and even financial. This means we need to begin to change how we live our lives. We need to stop unnecessarily wasting our resources. We need to conserve our personal resources and stop living deficit lifestyles. Our leaders started this in the past, and living a deficit lifestyle unfortunately became the way many Americans have chosen to live. This has become an attitude that is largely responsible for our massive and growing national debt. That attitude will need to change if we hope to make the changes we need to ensure our long-term survival. Fortunately, developing a deeper spiritual perspective makes it much simpler for us to make the necessary change in attitude and to change our actions for the better.

A spiritually open citizen knows the importance of clean, fresh, unadulterated food, and the importance of an adequate, healthful food supply for everyone.

As we're learning, healthful, unadulterated food is vital to a long and healthy life. The incidence of various diseases increases in direct correlation with chemical farming, introducing unnatural hybrids, and genetically manipulating foods to be chemical and pest resistant – all in the name of profit. Eating healthful, natural foods from infancy onward would be ideal, and it's very likely that people will be eating this way in a spiritual Republic. In addition, the cost of providing clean and healthful food is less than the amount we'd spend on medical care if we continue to poison ourselves with chemically-laden processed foods.

Distorting our food through genetic modification and unnatural hybridization brings with it considerable risks. There are always outcomes we can't predict, and we all know of many things that were initially deemed safe but were later recognized as harmful to our health (for example, radiation and cigarettes). We can very easily avoid the dangers to our health from frankenfoods by not focusing on profit and yield, and shifting our focus to providing the most healthful food possible for the population.

Industrial agricultural businesses will have to change their ways, but it's still feasible for them to farm healthfully and earn a profit. Until they change their ways, however, we can send a direct message to them by growing our own gardens and purchasing as much food as possible from local organic farmers. This directly benefits your local farmers, and over time industrial agriculture will get the message and will have to adapt.

Spiritual citizens are calm, centered, and at peace.
Having our soul in control of our thoughts and actions, instead of our ego, changes our thoughts and behaviors. We become far less impulsive and take almost nothing as a personal attack. Those weaknesses come from the ego, so a spiritually awake person, with their soul in charge of their actions, will have far fewer ego-based reactions and will be much more in balance as a result. (See the section on Spirituality if you want a refresher.)

We experience far fewer wide emotional swings when the ego is in check and performing its proper function. As a result, we stay more in balance, and our "swings" away from balance remain narrow. Being in this state allows citizens of a spiritual Republic to interact with each other with much less strife, which leads to more cooperation and more peacefully resolved situations. As this continues, spiritual citizens become better able to work together in agreement toward common goals. This leads to more progress and growth in society.

A spiritually aware person continually seeks greater spiritual awareness and deeper spiritual understanding.
Most people who embark on a spiritual journey find that spirituality becomes integrated into their way of life. It becomes a life-long journey of self-discovery and self-improvement. Learning a spiritual perspective takes more effort at first, but by persistently focusing on spiritual growth we create a "habit" of perceiving things spiritually. Every event in our lives becomes an opportunity for growth, and we learn more and more from the world around us and the people we meet. In effect, we learn that our daily life *is* our spiritual life. At that point, we can learn to live our life as though it is a continuous meditation. We learn that each moment in our lives can lead us to a deep inner peace, and this leads to the state of *grace*.

A person with a deeply spiritual perspective acknowledges the spiritual nature of humanity and the world.
Having a deep spiritual perspective frequently leads to the realization that all the life on this world is interconnected in some way. From that point, it's easy to make the leap to accepting that the life on this world could also be connected to something unseen that we don't perceive with our physical senses. In other words, it becomes much easier to outgrow the blind faith and trust taught by religious organizations and to truly accept that God exists, God created this universe, and that we are a spiritual facet of our Creator.

Once we embrace the understanding that we are spiritual beings and a part of our Creator, we come to understand that all of us have a part to play in God's creation. We learn to accept that each of us has a specific purpose to serve with our existence. We learn there is more to this world and its spiritual nature than we perceive with our five senses. Some of us even begin to learn how to perceive the deeper spiritual parts of our selves, each other, and the world around us. This spiral of upward growth continues as we learn more about our true nature and true spiritual origins.

121

****

I know all of this may seem idyllic, and actually attaining a spiritual Republic may seem out of reach, but it is genuinely within reach and closer than most of us would think. Developing a spiritual Republic is a process, and each step along the way brings us closer to our goal. Keep in mind that every positive step, no matter how small, still results in improvements that benefit everyone. Small improvements over time accumulate into significant positive change.

Small, incremental improvements bring our society closer to having universal spiritual laws as a part of its foundation. A true spiritual Republic has universal spiritual laws as its foundation, and those spiritual laws become woven into all aspects of society. As the universal laws permeate all levels, the need for external governmental laws naturally diminishes. This progression ultimately leads to a strong, stable, enduring spiritual Republic.

On the surface, a true spiritual Republic may appear to be what some might call a "utopia." There are, however, significant differences between a spiritual Republic and a utopia. The difference is that most utopias as defined by the authors who have described them are controlled by the government doling out resources so all citizens have the same things and want for nothing - and are therefore "equal." What utopian thinkers don't seem to realize is that a true utopia *cannot* come from a government and government legislation. It *must* come from the people. In a spiritual Republic there is absolute equality of opportunity, but each citizen is personally responsible for grasping that opportunity. Each person also has the *choice* of how much effort they wish to put forth, knowing that their effort directly affects the result they get. Someone who is capable and yet refuses to put in the necessary effort to be independent has no business expecting anyone else who "has more" to take care of him when he is physically able to take care of himself. There is no reward for laziness in a spiritual Republic. There is only reward for effort. People's efforts, and the tangible results from them, are the economic engine that drives modern society.

As a result, there is a distinct difference between the economy we have today and the economy of a spiritual Republic. The economy of today is driven by profit, and that tends to keep the focus on short-term operations and reducing all operational costs to a minimum. However, the economic driving force in a spiritual Republic is not maximizing profits; it's maximizing *value*. Maximizing value takes a longer-term business view. Keeping those values, and the long-term view, will allow a spiritual Republic to stay strong and viable for many centuries, and it will continue to evolve and improve over time. A true spiritual Republic can exist in perpetuity because the attributes of such a Republic are consistent with fundamental human values.

****

A spiritual Republic will be very strong, internally and externally. It will resist all attempts to tear it down by any force, whether by an external enemy or internal infiltrators, malcontents, or even corrupt elected officials. Most residents of a spiritual Republic will not be apathetic "sheeple." Instead, they'll be directly involved in or concerned about the daily affairs of the Republic, and will not accept any graft or corruption in any government officials. Corrupt officials will immediately be recalled or fired, and replaced with someone of true ethics who will listen to and follow the will of their constituents.

A true and functional spiritual Republic will be one of the highest forms of government we have ever seen on this planet; perhaps even the highest form. It's probable that other countries will take notice of this form of government, and that their citizens will want this type of government as well. The spiritual Republic form of government could very well spread around the world and come to be the most pervasive form of government on Earth. In this way the spiritual Republic could spread, creating more prosperous and peaceful countries throughout the world. In time, the spiritual Republic will dominate – not by conquest, but by *ideals*.

Part Five: Ideas for a spiritual Charter to be added to our Constitution

Some people claim the Constitution is an old, outmoded document that has served its purpose and no longer applies to life in America. I say they're wrong. Much of it was written to address the events happening at that time, but the root principles in the Declaration and Constitution still apply today. I think we can add to these root principles to include a deeper level of spirituality that applied in the past, still applies today, and will apply into the future.

Adding these principles as a Charter would be fairly simple and wouldn't involve amending the Constitution. These are spiritual principles that will ensure our liberty and help to maintain the strength and durability of our spiritual Republic.

The individual in a spiritual Republic is sovereign. All other entities exist to protect or improve the life of all individuals. The rights and liberties for all individuals are the same.
This eliminates all protected classes since none will be needed. Everyone will have the same protected rights as everyone else. These rights will be limited to actual persons and not available to business entities. No individual rights will be superseded by the rights of any business. After all, people are far more important than any business.

All individuals recognize that self-responsibility is paramount.
As our spiritual perspective deepens, we become more conscious of the importance of self-responsibility. We come to understand that it is no one else's responsibility to take care of us or manage our lives. Expecting someone else to assume responsibility for our lives directly opposes the Universal Law of Liberty. This also means that those who choose to take responsibility for others against their wishes and control them are directly opposing a Universal Law that is encoded into the fabric of our universe.

Along with self-responsibility comes the spiritually-based desire to help others who are in genuine need; those who have taken full responsibility for their life and actions, but who have fallen short due to circumstances beyond their control. People in these

125

circumstances will get the help they need without any government mandate or interference. The people who will run into problems are people with an entitlement mentality; people who expect others to take care of them as though it's a right, and who are often in dire circumstances due to many poor choices on their part. People in this situation haven't truly taken responsibility for their lives and done all they can to help themselves. Many people in this situation have squandered opportunities and expect others to pick up the slack. Individuals in this situation rely on government assistance, but it's typically government interference that lets them get away with this behavior repeatedly. A community choosing to voluntarily help someone can demand some effort and some evidence that the person receiving the help is working to improve their situation.

Each individual has the right to their personal point of view. No individual has the right to coerce another into believing their point of view.
Your spiritual viewpoint is perfect for your level of spiritual development. It's a product of many things; all those things have something in common, and that's *you*. Your point of view is highly personalized and is not perfect for everyone else, or even *anyone* else. This is true for everyone, and that's why we're all in some ways right in our beliefs. Other people have their own perspective and they're entitled to their point of view just as much as you are entitled to yours. That's why it's a spiritual error to try to get others to believe exactly as we believe. What we want to do is share our points of view with others and listen to theirs. In that way we learn from each other.

This brings up a good question: Are there points of view that are more right than other perspectives? Yes, in a sense. We learn broader perspectives from others or from our own experiences. Although our perspective is perfect for where we are spiritually, it's not *complete*. There is always more for us to learn and that's how we grow. Some people on Earth have learned deeper perspectives than others and have chosen to share those expanded points of view with others. These people are *spiritual teachers*. When you're learning from a spiritual teacher, be sure you don't dismiss anything they tell you out of hand without giving it real consideration. If you don't at least consider it you could be throwing away many learning opportunities that will help you deepen your own point of view.

All individuals will respect the property of another, will do their best to honor all their agreements, and will conduct their affairs with truthfulness, honesty, and integrity.

You'll find all of these attributes in someone with a truly spiritual perspective. They're a natural part of our spiritual development and stem from our Soul controlling our lives rather than the ego being in charge. This is because it's natural for your Soul to be truthful and honest, to have integrity, and to respect other people and their property. With our Soul controlling our lives we make each choice for the highest good of all. With that as our standard, it becomes very easy to do everything you agree to do since doing so provides a large measure of good for other people around you.

Each individual will be encouraged to embrace self-respect and will treat other individuals with respect and courtesy.

This statement seems fairly self-explanatory.

All individuals recognize that cultural differences exist, and agree to honor those differences.

Just as we, as individuals, have different perspectives, each culture has beliefs and practices that the members choose to follow. People are free to make a choice and practice the customs of any culture in which they feel comfortable. Everyone should feel free to practice any customs they wish to as long as those customs don't have a negative impact on others. It is, however, important to remember that practicing the customs of another culture should not negatively affect American culture in the process. To do so would cause harm to the spiritual Republic and would need to be addressed and corrected.

The primary functions of government are to protect its citizens and their rights and liberties. Secondary functions of government include providing for national defense and establishing and maintaining the infrastructure necessary for our society: roadways, power generation and distribution, clean, healthful water, and waste disposal. Funds to operate and perform these functions shall be generated by a 1% national sales tax, a graduated flat income tax, and import/export duties. All other powers are delineated in the Constitution and powers not enumerated in the Constitution remain with the State governments and the people.

This statement seems self-explanatory.

127

The U.S. government will be held accountable for the cost of its operations. The government will confine its activities to those already stated, will operate within reasonable limits of expense, and will operate within the limits of revenue collected annually. No deficit spending is permitted except during times of declared war.

This seems as though it should be reasonably obvious and it is the way our forefathers managed our country. We need to return to this system and this country needs to live within its means. Regardless of all the "it's not that easy" or "it's complicated" arguments, we need to do it. Period.

The graduated flat income tax applies to all citizens. There are no loopholes, exemptions, deductions beyond the standard gradations, and there is no double taxation.

We've all heard the line about the rich paying "their fair share." I have to ask: how is a progressive tax *fair?* The government wants more money from people who make more, and that's OK if everyone who is taxed is taxed at essentially the same rate. Where it ceases to be fair is when the tax *rate* increases as income increases. There are two basic problems here. One is this underlying and unspoken premise: when many people think of "rich" they also think *dishonest*. While it's true in some cases, there are many wealthy people who earned their money honestly. Simply put, if it were anyone but the government, taking that much away from those who have earned it would be stealing and fraud.

The other significant factor is that most of the people negatively affected by this type of system are people who have a fairly high income (perhaps doctors or lawyers, etc.) but who aren't actually rich. They often have high debt ratios due to having education loans, car loans, a mortgage, and all the regular expenses of life like the rest of us. People in that situation have worked hard to get to where they are and work hard to earn their salary. Many probably have several hundred thousand dollars in outstanding student loans. Why should the government take more money from them because they have a high income? The answer is they shouldn't, but the government has the power so they can and they do. People who are very wealthy (arbitrarily, let's say with over $10 million in assets) are troubled less by the high tax rate than are high income earners without significant assets. The system doesn't distinguish between them, and besides all that there is this simple truth: excess taxation is a sign of oversized government and mismanaged government finances.

On the other side of the coin are people who pay no tax and receive government credits. Many of them need financial help and they'll still get it under a graduated flat tax system. Everyone who earns enough income to actually pay tax will have that income taxed at the same low rate as everyone else. Any other system – including the progressive tax system we have right now – is just another form of legalized government robbery.

No inherited funds will be taxed, excepting funds that have not been previously taxed.
Since doubly taxing funds is another form of legalized government robbery, it genuinely seems that is something our government should not be doing. The only assets in an estate that should be taxed are assets held in retirement accounts that haven't been previously taxed.

Elected officials and all public offices shall have a single term of service.
The terms of service for Federal elected positions shall be: President – one six-year term. Senate – one six-year term, with one-third of the Senate renewed every two years. Senators will be appointed by the executive branch of their home state, and may be recalled by their state legislature at any time during their term of service. House of Representatives: one four-year term with one third of the House being renewed every two years by popular election. Supreme Court justices will have a single five year term. Any Directorates appointed by the President will have a six year term and will be appointed mid-term in each Presidency.

All public offices will have specific criteria for experience and performance.
All public offices shall be filled by citizens who meet specified experience and performance criteria, and who have clearly demonstrated a high degree of honesty and integrity in managing their personal affairs.

Any person in any public office, whether elected or hired, who is found guilty of graft, corruption, or any illegal activities will be immediately and permanently removed from said position and will be subject to mandatory incarceration of a commensurate duration. Such persons will be permanently barred from any future public service position or office. No one found guilty of graft, corruption, or any illegal activities will be eligible to hold any public office, whether elected, appointed, or hired.

The armed forces of the United States exist solely to protect the interests of the United States and its citizens, and never for conquest.
A spiritual Republic has no interest in violently conquering any other nation and would never consider doing so. The military might of a spiritual Republic will only be used to oppose those who take up arms against us. The spiritual Republic form of government may in time sweep the globe, but every new spiritual Republic formed will come from the desire for liberty and the choice of each country's citizens. Some countries may choose to not embrace a spiritual Republic, and that's OK. As long as it is their choice, and they don't threaten the United States or our allies, people of other nations can live as they choose to live.

Crime is not accepted in the United States, and all crime will be firmly punished.
Anyone convicted of any crime will lose all individual rights as a citizen for the duration of their punishment. The sentence for all punishments dispensed by a judge shall be fully served. Well-behaved prisoners will be rewarded with greater privileges as appropriate. Any repeat offender who returns to incarceration for the third time will remain incarcerated for the remainder of their natural life without parole. Execution without appeal will be considered a just punishment for criminals convicted of any sufficiently heinous crime as determined by a judge and jury.

Every individual has the right to defend their person and others from those who threaten and intend bodily harm.
This should *never* be challenged. No government professing liberty should ever tell its citizens that they have no right to defend their life or the life of their loved ones. This is a Natural Right that the government is not truly empowered to usurp. The government may strip this protection from its citizens, but in doing so the

130

government will have broken a spiritual law and it will have created a law it has no authority to create.

Legal immigration will be permitted as defined in United States policy.
The United States retains all rights to specify the criteria that need to be met for legal immigration, and to limit or restrict all immigration. Illegal immigration is a crime and will be punished as a crime.

Part Six: How to become a Spiritual Republic from where we are today

This section alone could probably fill a small encyclopedia. What I'll provide here are some basic things we can readily accomplish that will get us on the right path – the path of transforming America as it is today into a spiritual Republic. It's important to remember that everything in this section can be readily achieved. There is nothing here we can't do, and the accumulated effects of doing each of these things is to set America on the path to becoming a spiritual Republic.

The major barriers to most of these ideas will be apathy, closed-off perspectives, and people entrenched in positions of power. Many people don't like change; most of the current group of people in power are part of the problem and won't like many of these solutions. As a result, we'll need to elect new representatives wise enough to see the bigger picture and strong enough to support Americans and take these actions.

As I've stated before, it will also be critical to have more people developing true spiritual awareness through spiritual growth – and willing to teach these foundational spiritual principles to their children. This will ensure that the changes we make for the better remain in place and aren't undermined in the future by greedy self-interests.

Let's briefly cover how we can begin to change our current political system to one that can endure as long as America can stand as a spiritual Republic – which could potentially be millennia.

Some necessary political steps:

Americans with deeper spiritual understanding – including some people reading this book – will need to take action and seek a public office.
There is no doubt that our current political system attracts certain types of people. However, it often fails to attract the *best* people for elected positions. That's really no surprise. Most people don't want to deal with the political climate that has come to engulf

133

Washington. While this is completely understandable, it's also something that will need to change.

Unfortunately, many spiritually aware people want no part of Washington politics. Equally unfortunately, changing Washington from the outside will be exceedingly difficult, if it's possible at all. This means we'll need more spiritually-focused candidates in every election from this point forward. If you believe or know you are spiritually aware, I encourage you to seek a public office at whatever level fits your qualifications. We can change the system from the inside, a bit at a time, until we have a majority of elected representatives who are at least spiritually open. Then our government representatives will be able to work together for the benefit of Americans and the United States as a whole. Yes, it will be difficult and take time; however, this is a crucial step in order to reach the goal of transforming America into a true spiritual Republic.

Purge Congress by voting for NO incumbents who have been in office for longer than 2 terms for at least 3 election cycles.
We **must** break the power cycle in Washington. A simple way to do this is to eliminate all career politicians, and we can do this over 3 or 4 election cycles. It should be fairly obvious that the long-standing members of Congress and the Senate have not made a significant positive difference. In fact, things have gotten worse for the country under their leadership. If they had made a positive difference, this country and its citizens would be far better off today than we currently are. Since corrupt career politicians are a part of the problem, we can unify our efforts and eliminate a great deal of corruption by purging long-standing Representatives and Senators.

The reason this will decrease corruption is simple: it takes time to amass power in Washington. Time and *deals*. Removing the career politicians also removes the power structures they've assembled over the years. By doing this, we are making it easier for novice representatives – who, if we're careful, will be mainly *statesmen* – to enter bills that will amend our laws and Constitution to create term limits or, ideally, a single-term representative government (more details on this are coming up later in this section).

Since amending our Constitution to include term limits is an important part of this transition, we'll need to elect candidates who, as part of their platform, support term limits for all politicians and appointees. We already know the existing politicians won't pass legislation that forces them out of office. Since career politicians will never voluntarily do this, we absolutely need to replace them with statesmen who will.

Before we wrap up this section, I'd also like to mention again that it's essential to elect *trustworthy* representatives. The actions of someone who is trustworthy match their words. If your state or area elects a lying politician instead of a truthful statesman, at minimum they should not be re-elected. Ideally, pushing for a recall and special election would send the message that "business as usual" in Washington will no longer be tolerated by the American people.

Restore State checks on the Federal government by repealing the 17th Amendment.

Repealing the 17th Amendment is essential. This is the Amendment that changed how Senators are brought into office. The Founders and Framers intended to have the State legislatures appoint Senators. Restoring this gives the States the opportunity to begin the process of taking back the powers the Federal government has usurped, and this usurpation may not have happened at all if the Senators were still appointed by the State. The Senate was originally intended to represent State governments as Federal representatives of the State's population. Changing the method of electing Senators to popular vote cut the State governments out of the power loop, and one of the checks in place to limit Federal power was by the States appointing Senators. We can all clearly see what this change has led to: a seriously bloated government that can grow virtually unchecked and which is seeking greater and greater control over citizen's lives.

Article 1, Section 3 of the Constitution specifies how Senators are to be appointed. Here is the text of that section:

> "The Senate of the United States shall be composed of two Senators from each State, chosen by the Legislature thereof, for six Years; and each Senator shall have one Vote."

This was later changed by Amendment 17, and here is the text of Amendment 17 that pertains to selecting Senators (passed in 1913):

> "The Senate of the United States shall be composed of two Senators from each State, elected by the people thereof, for six years; and each Senator shall have one vote. The electors in each State shall have the qualifications requisite for electors of the most numerous branch of the State legislatures."

Restoring this process to its proper procedure restores the States' abilities to constrain the Federal government when it oversteps its bounds. Every administration since this Amendment was ratified has overstepped its bounds and taken power that is not granted to the Federal government by the Constitution. Restoring the original process will help bring the government under control, and this will help to improve the country and to reduce the size of the Federal government as the United States gradually becomes a spiritual Republic.

The new members of Congress must institute *singular* terms of service by Constitutional amendment.
There are an enormous number of benefits that arise from having elected officials serve a single term. Although there is no real way to prove this, I suspect that single terms are what the Framers originally had in mind. There were some distinct benefits from the continuity of having George Washington serve two terms, but that was when this country was just newly formed. We're not at that point now, and career politicians have largely used the system to greedily amass power and wealth. It's time to change that. It's time to consider these single term lengths, with no re-elections:

Recommended terms:
>President/VP: 6yrs
>Senate: 6yrs, but appointed by State legislatures as per the Constitution (repeal 17th amendment)
>House: 4 yrs, voted in by popular election
>Supreme Court Justices: 5 yrs (instead of life as it is now)
>Cabinet members and appointed Directorates: A single 6 yr term appointed at mid-term in each Presidency.

A single-term system eliminates career politicians. The people who will be serving will most likely have had other productive careers. They may be at the end of their career and want to contribute their accumulated experience to the whole. Or they may be seeking a way to apply their present skills to benefit others before moving forward onto a different path. Either way, the majority of their experience is *life* experience and not political experience. Life experience spent among fellow members of society will help keep potential candidates in touch with the realities of life and up to date with the changes and current challenges in our society.

As mentioned before, having a single term removes most of the incentive to make back-door deals to amass power. This will absolutely benefit constituents since their representative's only purpose will be to do the job they were elected to do. Naturally, as more spiritually-focused candidates get elected over time, our current government will evolve into a government that is service-oriented and ethical.

A tremendous benefit of having a single-term system is that no working time will be lost from campaigning for re-election. Instead, the entire time in office will be spent doing the job they've been elected – and that they're being paid – to do. Running for re-election also affects many decisions made while in office. In some cases it's likely that some politicians didn't do what they knew was right because doing so could have cost them re-election. Having a single term eliminates this problem entirely.

Eliminate the Party system, and replace the parties with a Board of Elections.
It should be clear to everyone who has been paying attention that the party system we now have is a serious barrier to real progress. It may have served a purpose in the past, but this system has run its course and it's time for a significant change. That change is to eliminate political parties and the divisiveness they cause.

There will obviously be extreme resistance to that from the entrenched parties, but we can collectively take action to overcome that resistance. Once again, it will start with who we elect as representatives. We'll need to elect ·forward-thinking representatives – quite possibly independents outside the party system – who see the problems with the system and who are willing to take steps to change this broken system. We need to vote for candidates who aren't afraid of positive change, and who are willing to support the changes we need to improve our country and its political climate.

We can successfully replace the parties with a Bureau of Elections. This naturally non-partisan bureau can begin reforming our system by first establishing accurate and realistic job descriptions for each position. Any candidate who does not meet the necessary qualifications can't run for the position, and any candidate who is qualified can run in the primaries. Candidates who accrue enough votes in the primaries can move forward to elections. In this way the voting public can focus on the candidate's positions on the issues. Candidates are then free to express their own views without feeling obligated to support a specific political party position. There are surely many details to work out, but these are steps that we can take to change our flawed and failing system.

Another factor to consider in campaigning is campaign financing. With the current state of political advertising, and all the negative ads that pollute our radio listening and television watching, I'm sure many people would agree it's time for a change. In today's world, it's very possible for a candidate to get their campaign message out via the internet and on local TV and radio (via interviews) at relatively low cost. Perhaps it's time to limit candidates to public funds, or eliminate donations from businesses and only allow donations from individuals. In this way, each individual is free to support the candidate of their choice and no candidate is directly supported by any business.

Wealthy supporters may still make contributions, but those contributions would have to be personal and not business in order to be allowed. There is plenty of room here for additional new ideas, but the basic premise still stands: it's time to eliminate political parties and stop the divisiveness they cause.

Change the way Bills are presented in the House and Senate.
The way Bills are presented and processed in Congress is a huge part of the problem with our system. Under the current system, Bills have complex language and are written to be excessively long –

ensuring that virtually no one actually reads them. Add to that the provision for combining unrelated Bills and tacking on amendments, and you have a rotten system that promotes graft and corruption in many ways.

There are a few simple things we can change that will go a long way to help this problem, and all of these changes can be made without affecting the Constitution. First, write Bills in plain English. If there is nothing to hide, simple, direct, concise language will make this process easier on everyone. Next, stop combining unrelated pieces of legislation and stop adding in unrelated amendments. This only serves the purpose of getting unwanted legislation and unwanted amendments passed because they're attached to legislation everyone essentially agrees with. This is, simply put, a fraudulent use of our legislation process. Any piece of legislation that can't stand on its own and pass is generally unwanted and probably unnecessary legislation originating from a special interest. Lastly, with all the Bills in plain language and only related legislation combined, it should be simple to meet this last requirement: all Representatives and Senators must actually *read the Bills*. This seems so obvious, yet it's still not regularly done. Simplifying the system will solve this problem too. In this way, all representatives will know exactly why they are voting for or against the legislation.

Stop Federal deficit spending.
This seems so plain and simple that it shouldn't even warrant its own section. But somehow our politicians got into the habit of kicking the can down the road. Well, if they do that long enough, the can they're kicking will wind up being kicked into the sewer, and that's exactly what's happening now in the United States. Our country is *insanely* in debt, and the politicians keep up the spending spree. Anyone with just a few IQ points stashed in their head knows that this can't go on forever. We're now on the brink of insolvency, and the 500+ elected representatives in this country responsible for creating this mess have chained all Americans to a mountain of debt most didn't want. In a real sense, the massive debt we're all on the hook for didn't really do much. It didn't benefit everyone. Instead it benefited relatively few Americans, rewarded a few "elite" members of society for screwing the rest of us over, and helped out some foreign nations – some of whom are hostile to the U.S.!

A huge part of this problem comes from the government being too large and usurping many State powers, robbing some of our liberties in the process. We basically all agree that the Federal government wastes a lot of money, *but it's our money they're wasting.* Many of our elected officials believe we gave it to them to spend, and they're happy to keep spending as long as we keep ponying up. It's time to take a strong, firm stand and elect representatives who will stop hurting hard-working Americans. It's time that we demand our government be responsible with our funds and demonstrate responsible stewardship with our finances, our efforts, and our future.

We can start with a balanced budget. Tell the government we require them to stop raising the debt ceiling and start living within its means. If they don't, vote all the representatives who keep stabbing us in the back out of office at the next election. Or, if enough people in your State agree, recall them on the spot and call for a special election to replace them. Doing this just a few times will surely get the attention of all representatives, and many will fall into line as a result.

This country is no longer in a position to try and rescue the world. We've spent ourselves into the poor house, so it is well past time to make some vital changes. If we don't, we will essentially be at the mercy of a number of hostile nations, hoping they don't pull the trigger. But who knows? Maybe that has been the plan all along for at least some of our leaders.

Assume responsibility for paying down the national debt instead of passing it down the line.
We lightly touched on this in the previous section. Now let's take a closer look at this.

The national debt is *huge*. And it's growing rapidly. Even so, we don't need to keep making it worse with deficit spending, and that's the easiest change we can make. After we have a balanced budget, we need to generate a healthy surplus to begin repaying the debt. Repaying it will take decades, and perhaps over a century, but it is essential to begin shrinking the debt as soon as possible. In a real sense, we are to some degree at the mercy of our debt holders. China holds a fair proportion of our debt (as of December 2014, almost $1.5 TRILLION dollars of it), and at the moment they don't want the U.S. to collapse or their economy could collapse as well. They're not strong enough yet to survive us defaulting, but they eventually will be. You can be sure that is when the debt will be called in for repayment.

Defaulting on debt to China will likely lead to war, so if we don't find some way to begin paying them off the Chinese may eventually offer another way to settle up: some form of trade. Unfortunately, what they may want in trade could be something we won't want to part with. In such a serious scenario, it's entirely possible that they may demand U.S. property, such as Alaska or Hawaii in exchange. This may seem impossible, but it certainly could be the direction we're heading if we don't get our house in order.

Naturally, part of getting our house in order will involve *significantly* reducing government spending. There are numerous ways to accomplish this. Some are obvious and some will need more research. This topic alone could be the subject of several large books.

On the flip side of that coin is properly increasing government revenue. Simply raising taxes on everyone is not the answer. The real answer is paying our debt down by fueling *prosperity*. Let's make the United States a place where businesses want to be. Let's increase tax revenue by increasing business revenues. In that way, growth will enable us to pay our debts and will help Americans become more individually prosperous as well. A prosperous America is a strong America. This route clearly seems to be the best choice. Of course, to follow this path will mean eliminating unnecessary bureaucratic regulations and creating a favorable tax climate here in the U.S.. Make it more attractive for businesses to remain rather than sending their operations and jobs overseas. It won't be as difficult to accomplish this as it may seem on the surface. The hardest part of this will be fixing our disastrous tax code. It won't be easy, but it must be done. It's one of the steps we need to take to ensure future generations are still Americans and not some other nationality.

Responsibly managing our government by using annual revenues instead of debt financing is a principle that has been with us since the inception of this nation. President John Adams, in his State of the Union address on November 22, 1797, had this to say on that topic:

> "Since the decay of the feudal system, by which the public defense was provided for chiefly at the expense of individuals, the system of loans has been introduced, and as no nation can raise within the year by taxes sufficient sums for its defense and military operations in time of war. The sums loaned and debts contracted have necessarily become the subjects of what have been called funding systems. The consequences arising from the continual accumulation of public debts in other countries ought to admonish us to be careful to prevent their growth in our own. *The national defense must be provided for as well as the support of Government; but both should be accomplished as much as possible by immediate taxes, and as little as possible by loans."* (emphasis added)

If we begin again to adhere to these founding principles, we can operate our government within our means and at a minimum reduce the burden of debt that *we* created, instead of weighing down future generations with a responsibility that is not in any way truly theirs.

Eliminate all Federal and State subsidies and bailouts.
This probably seems harsh on the surface, but it actually brings out an important point: if a business enterprise can't be profitable on its own, it serves no real purpose in a capitalist market. In a free market system, a business that can't provide more in value than it costs to operate will naturally fail. This is entirely appropriate, and getting governments involved in rescuing unprofitable businesses is not at all what our government is for or should be doing. Following this course of action to perpetually sustain unprofitable businesses is essentially stealing profits from solvent businesses in the name of government "taxation." This directly reduces America's overall prosperity and true productivity.

This doesn't mean that a new business that generates a new product shouldn't get help to get off the ground. If the product will benefit people's lives and the business can eventually operate profitably, then providing funding to launch new businesses and new products is a proper use of government funding or lending. What we need to eliminate or change are businesses that couldn't exist without subsidies, and subsidies that artificially reduce costs of supplies or commodities. Money for perpetual subsidies comes from profitable businesses; those businesses could be made more profitable, and their employees more prosperous, if they weren't being forced to support a business that would fail on its own. The market will determine what businesses are providing value to consumers; government intervention in this case drags the system down and doesn't allow the free market economy to operate the way it is designed to.

Similarly, the government should not be providing bailouts to businesses that are failing due to mismanagement. Doing so simply rewards the management for screwing up and penalizes taxpayers – both businesses and individuals – forcing them to pay to clean up someone else's mess (a mess that can lead to significant profit for the guilty). That is not good financial stewardship, and violates the spiritual principle of self-responsibility. Fortunately, inappropriate bailouts and similar events will be a rare occurrence in a spiritual Republic.

Instead of a bailout, let the guilty parties accept responsibility for their actions and let them use existing means (bankruptcy courts, for example) to properly resolve their situation. If that means the business managers have to explain to shareholders why their money is gone, so be it. Doing so is part of spiritually accepting self-responsibility.

Some readers are no doubt wondering: what about farmers?

Farm subsidies for small to moderate sized farms run by families will clearly need to remain in place for now, although they will not be needed forever. Large and profitable industrialized farms should not receive subsidies at all. In the long run, with our produce being kept more local and being less chemical-laden, family farms will eventually be able to operate at a profit. Most of this will come about without having to raise prices exorbitantly because smaller farms will be able to operate with lower costs.

Right now, farmers have to sell their produce at drastically reduced prices, often at or below their cost (which is why subsidies exist). As our perception of food changes and more people want to eat fresh local food, costs in transportation, storage, and packaging will decrease. Most farmers will be able to sell directly to retail or through food co-ops, giving them a substantially greater profit margin. It will be possible in many areas to have indoor produce markets in co-ops that represent local farmers at a reasonable overhead. In this way we can ensure that the people who work hard to grow healthful food can also make a decent living without government subsidies. I suspect many farmers would much rather farm at a profit instead of depending on the government.

This change would at first happen in rural areas, then spread into larger cities. Although it will take time, eventually smaller farms will be able to meet some of the needs of inner city families as well. Perhaps vertical farming can be explored to fill the gap in urban areas. Society will benefit from cleaner, fresher, and more healthful food. People will slowly become healthier as their bodies purge the harmful agricultural chemicals currently in use. Children will grow up healthier, and health care costs will come down. All from something as simple as buying healthier local foods.

Decrease the size of the government and the number of regulatory agencies (and regulations) as the population and businesses become more self-responsible and self-regulating.
It seems clear that, based on our experiences, having a large government that controls most of our lives strangles prosperity and does very little to ensure greater safety. In fact, a prosperous America has far more potential to provide greater security to its citizens than does a weakened America drowning in debt and overregulation. A prosperous America is a strong America, and the Founding Fathers knew this quite well.

Once again, President John Adams demonstrated that this idea was well-accepted during the beginnings of our nation, and it is a principle that still holds true today. Here is another statement that supports the importance of prosperity, again from his State of the Union address on November 22, 1797:

"The commerce of the United States is essential, if not to their existence, at least to their comfort, their growth, prosperity, and happiness. The genius, character, and habits of the people are highly commercial. Their cities have been formed and exist upon commerce. Our agriculture, fisheries, arts, and manufactures are connected with and depend upon it. *In short, commerce has made this country what it is, and it can not be destroyed or neglected without involving the people in poverty and distress.* (emphasis added) Great numbers are directly and solely supported by navigation. The faith of society is pledged for the preservation of the rights of commercial and sea faring no less than of the other citizens. Under this view of our affairs, I should hold myself guilty of a neglect of duty if I forbore to recommend that *we should make every exertion to protect our commerce and to place our country in a suitable posture of defense as the only sure means of preserving both.*"(emphasis added)

Our society is indeed founded on commerce, and we have weakened our financial base with government overregulation. Over time, as the degree of spiritual awareness in our citizens grows, there will be far less need for government regulation. At that future time it will be fairly easy to reduce the size of the government as much as is needed. However, we need to take some action *today* and can't wait for some future time. We need less strangling business regulation *now* if we are to preserve our nation and restore it to its true stature as a Republic. This is a vital step in our growth as a nation, and it is a vital step for us to develop into a spiritual Republic.

****

We will need to change a number of our perspectives and policies as a nation, and as a people, in order to transition the United States into a true spiritual Republic. Doing so will bring about the growth that will transform our faltering nation into one that stands as an inspiration to other nations. As a spiritual Republic, the United States will be a powerful force that could change the world for the better; and, over time, could even unify the world.

Some other necessary changes:

In addition to the previously-mentioned political changes, we'll need to take these steps to help transform the United States into a spiritual Republic:

We need to stop playing world police.

Let's be clear, right up front: this does NOT mean ignoring threats to the safety of our country and its citizens. However, the citizens of a spiritual Republic recognize that people in other countries may choose to live differently than we do. It's their right to do so, and we would have no business interfering in their lives if they keep to themselves and don't threaten the United States or its allies – even if that country erupts into civil war.

We will not be invading other countries because they disagree with us and we "think" they may have weapons of mass destruction. We won't invade other nations because their leaders make threats against the U.S.. We will strongly respond to any aggressive *actions* these countries take after making threats, even if those actions are directed at another nation. We will assist our allies if they're threatened. Beyond that, we simply will not interfere with the citizens of another country and how they choose to live. They have the right to live as they choose, just as we do. If we want other nations to consider the benefits of being a spiritual Republic, then our best choice is to act with honor and integrity and be the best example that we can be. Let other country's citizens see that example, and make it known they want these benefits for themselves. Then we are free to help other countries without violence and without asserting our will over theirs.

One situation that could be difficult to live with would be countries run by tyrants. Even in that circumstance, we are obligated not to act until we can determine for certain that their citizens want to end the tyranny but need help to do so. We are free to help once we know they are being coerced, not living as they choose, and the majority of citizens support their country becoming a spiritual Republic. We would be spiritually obligated to help end the tyranny and free the populace to live their lives in accord with their own choices.

Protect our nation's borders and eliminate as much illegal immigration as possible.
Immigration may be a touchy point for some people, and a spiritual Republic would not seek to end all immigration. We would, however, put great effort into stopping *illegal* immigration.

Anyone from another country who wishes to move to the United States has legal channels available to them. Entering this country illegally is a crime, and criminals are simply not welcome in our spiritual Republic. Some of the illegal immigrants may have been law-abiding in their country, but entering this country illegally means they don't value the laws of our country and that is not acceptable to the citizens of this Republic. In addition, some illegal immigrants are known criminals in their home country and are fleeing the law. Those criminals are not welcome here, so we will need to firmly secure our borders against illegal entry.

Not securing our borders creates many problems, and often these problems need to be handled by the States bordering other nations. In our case the primary immigration problem is from Mexico. The border States have to bear the brunt of the problems that come from the Federal government ignoring illegal immigration and not taking sufficient action to solve the problem. This is wrong to ask of the States since it is a national security issue, and the Federal government in a spiritual Republic will support the States in their attempts to secure their borders by providing appropriate resources and personnel to solve this growing problem.

As a spiritual Republic, we would see illegal immigration as a threat to our country for reasons already stated. Once we take the actions needed to secure our borders, we can then address how to solve the problem of illegal immigrants who are already here.

It seems reasonable that all illegal immigrants who are employed, productive, and not criminals should be welcomed as visitors – provided they're willing to put in the time and effort to become true citizens of the United States if they wish to stay. Unemployed and unproductive illegal immigrants who have no real skills can be offered training as a path to citizenship. If they're unwilling to accept training, or unwilling to work and be productive, then they'll be returned to their home country. Any illegal immigrant found to

147

be a criminal – whether in their own country or this one – will be deported and permanently barred from legal entry.

While all this may seem to some people to be harsh, it's necessary in order to protect our spiritual Republic from a potential threat.

Eliminate "protected" classes.
Individual rights are the primary rights in a spiritual Republic. Therefore, we won't need any protected classes since everyone, as an individual, has the same protected rights as everyone else. In a sense, the "individual" would be the only "protected" class since the government in a spiritual Republic is tasked with protecting the rights of each individual citizen.

By doing this, and by treating all individuals equally, discrimination has no basis upon which to exist. It's up to Americans to stop behaviors that create difference and separation if we want everyone to be treated equally. Some particular public figures often appear during specific types of unfortunate events that can be racially exploited, and their sole purpose is to create the appearances of separation and racial tension. They foment negative feelings and distort unfortunate events in order to perpetuate separation and discrimination. It's up to us, as Americans, to take away their power. Their power comes from us and the negative actions people choose to take in the name of perceived racism. In reality, stirring up those emotions and acting negatively, or even criminally, does tremendous harm to race relations and does no real good at all.

The simple answer to the majority of discrimination and racism is in unity. Act in ways that show unity with each other. Don't make assumptions about other people's motivations; be concerned only with your own motivations for taking the actions you choose to take. As more people refuse to be goaded into negative actions, and as fewer people make erroneous assumptions and then act as though they're true, the faster we'll be able to create a world in which every American is recognized first as an American citizen and not as a member of any other group. We're all people. Let's treat each other respectfully, courteously, and fairly. If we do this, we will never again need to recognize any "protected" class because we will all be treated equally – as Americans.

Simplify our tax code and make the IRS smaller and less powerful.
It should be obvious to anyone that a system that needs so many exemptions and deductions is clearly broken. So let's start over and re-create the IRS in a simpler and smaller form. What we need to do is fairly obvious. Instead of the crazy system we have now, which only grows more complex every year, we need to switch to a graduated flat tax system coupled with a small national sales tax.

There are many who would probably oppose a national sales tax, but it makes sense in various ways. I'll define what I mean, then look at an example that is likely to be fairly close to a final system that will work.

The first tax under this system is a 1% national sales tax. Food will be exempted from this tax but nothing else will. Therefore, people who spend more money will pay more sales tax. Note that this tax will NOT be deductible since that type of deduction won't exist under the revised system. Since this tax on its own won't provide enough revenue – at least for now and a part of the future – a graduated flat income tax will be needed as well.

The tax rate is fixed in a graduated flat tax. We'll use 15% as our example tax rate, although it's possible that 10% or 12% could be enough if used in conjunction with reduced government spending and a small national sales tax. However, the flat tax rate could probably be capped at 15%, and the government will need to operate within its means and not continue deficit spending. This 15% rate will apply to graduated personal income, business revenue, capital gains tax, retirement funds withdrawn before retirement or untaxed retirement funds passed on to descendents through an estate. There will be no other estate taxes besides the tax on previously untaxed inherited funds, no penalties on withdrawing retirement funds before retirement, and no tax on withdrawing IRA funds after retirement.

As an income tax, the 15% tax rate will only apply to a portion of a person's or family's income, and not the entire amount. A single exemption will be provided and based on family size. In our example, we'll use a $15K exemption for each adult, and a $5K exemption for each child. There will also be a cap of 10 individuals that qualify for an exemption. So a family of 12 people will have the same exemption as a family of 10. This is fair and reasonable because family size is a matter of choice. It's not reasonable to ask other people to help support someone else's children because they chose to have a very large family. Since the family has made the choice to exceed the exemption limit, they'll need to be sure their finances can support that choice. This falls under the spiritual principle of self-responsibility. Now let's look at this with some numbers.

Our example family has 2 adults and 3 children. Both parents work, and their combined income is $60K per year.

Income	$60,000
2 adult exemptions	-30,000
3 child exemptions	-15,000
Net taxable income	$15,000
Taxes	$2,250

The net effective Federal tax rate for our example family is 3.75% of their total income. Now let's look at this simple example using the current system and the tax year 2013. This will be a simplified example, but it will still convey the necessary information. In this example, we'll assume the family is filing a joint return, took the standard deduction, and put $2,000 into an IRA. Here's what we get when we run this information through a 1040:

Income	$60,000
IRA deduction	$2,000
Adjusted Gross Income	$58,000
Standard deduction	$12,200
Exemptions	$19,500
Taxable income	$26,300
Tax due	$3,049

As you can see, the current system would cost this family $799 *more* in taxes in 2013. Their Federal tax as a percentage of income would be 5.08%. I suspect these numbers are not way out of line, and this hypothetical scenario probably reflects a large number of actual families. As you can see from this brief example, a large number of middle-class American families would save some money on taxes every year with a graduated flat tax at 15%. Naturally, their savings will increase as the percentage drops. Tax savings grow as income grows. The country also benefits from a shorter and simpler tax code and fewer IRS regulations, resulting in decreased government operating expenses. Using this system, everyone pays their "fair share."

The graduated tax fills the gap between the revenue generated by the national sales tax and the total governmental operating cost. The flat tax percentage could decrease over time as America gets back on track and we successfully eliminate excess spending and excess government, and pay down our national debt.

Retirement account regulations will also change under this type of system. All retirement accounts will be funded with post-tax dollars since there is no complex combination of deductions, exemptions, and tax credits in a graduated flat-tax system. In addition, all funding limits will be removed on retirement accounts so people will be able to deposit as much as they choose to at any time. These changes are all in line with the spiritual principles of free will and self-responsibility. As mentioned above, funds withdrawn after retirement will not be subject to taxation.

Before we leave this topic, let's take a brief look at the effect of a 1% national sales tax for our hypothetical family. Let's say they didn't make any large purchases, such as a car. If their expenditures for household items, cell phones, and any other sales-tax items (food is excluded) were $20,000, which would be *a lot*, their additional tax would be $200. They'd still be $599 ahead for the year on their taxes. Would *you* want to give the government the extra $599, or keep it for yourself?

Reform our medical care system.
Affordable health care is important. However, forcing people to make purchases they don't want in order to subsidize other people's medical insurance may seem fine to our current government, but this would never happen in a spiritual Republic.

Our current government seems content to throw enormous sums of our tax dollars at broken programs just to keep them barely afloat. This is clearly a foolish way to operate. Yet the bureaucrats don't care much because it's not their money and the broken system doesn't affect them anyway. It's easy to make decisions for others when you don't have to live by them. Under those conditions, however, it seems that making *good* decisions is virtually impossible for many of today's politicians.

Although it's not a quick fix, reducing the cost of our medical care needs to begin with properly evaluating the system. We need to determine what works properly and what doesn't. We need to see what percentage of the tests performed have hidden legal reasons behind them rather than being medically necessary. We need to re-evaluate our society's prescription drugs as well. We need to put efforts into discovering what is causing the most common medical conditions instead of treating them once we have them. Many of these conditions may be resolved in a better way by lifestyle changes that reduce the likelihood of getting the disease. Not addressing underlying causes and covering up symptoms with medication is a foolish approach that is ultimately doomed to failure. It diminishes the patient's quality of life, and reducing symptoms without removing the cause means the problem is never resolved and will nearly always come back. While this is what many pharmaceutical companies surely want, this type of medical care essentially puts drug company profits ahead of people's well-being. Simply put, this is a travesty and needs to stop.

Clearly, not all drugs are a part of this trap. Most of the common drugs could very well be, however. Drugs like statins and high blood pressure medication are frequently covering up poor lifestyle choices people are making, and they'll ironically be able to, in many cases, live a *better* life by correcting the root issue instead of relying on drugs. Our medical system doesn't stand on its own, and there are three other huge factors that feed into the problems we have in our medical care system. These are: significant influence from our legal system, the damaging influence of insurance companies, and the absolute mess we've made of the food most people consume. We'll be considering each of those topics separately.

Another thing for people to consider is the value of many "alternative" therapies. Many medical professionals don't know much about them, and some doctors dismiss these alternatives as a result. This is unfortunate since some alternative therapies are often better at helping the body heal than many of the drugs dispensed – especially in cases needing lifestyle changes. Every form of treatment serves some purpose, and we need to, over time, create a unified approach that integrates all the best that each type of therapy has to offer. We can learn to develop a "whole person" approach that takes lifestyle and lifestyle choices into account, and match the best therapy to what each patient needs. Our life expectancies could substantially increase if we take this approach, along with living in a clean environment, eating clean, healthful food, drinking clean water, dropping harmful habits, and living a life without substantial stress.

Our medical insurance system needs an overhaul.
Our current medical insurance system is a significant part of our medical costs problem. This problem has been recognized for a long time. Too often medical professionals are limited in the care they can provide by what the patient's insurance company will reimburse. With the high cost of many tests and procedures, doctors know that people simply can't afford to pay for expensive tests out of pocket.

Insurance companies do need to survive as businesses, and they need profit to survive. It's important for them to recognize, however, that the business founders made the choice to enter that specific business. They also need to recognize that, due to the nature of their business, trying to generate excessive profits is only going to hurt the people they've agreed to cover.

A workable medical insurance system requires a close, interactive relationship between the patient, their doctor, and the insurer. It may also involve other practitioners as well. This system requires that the doctor be given the latitude to order whatever tests may be necessary, and to perform any procedures the patient needs and consents to. It also requires that the doctors be more aware of the costs associated with these procedures, and to use the most effective tools at their disposal that are appropriate for the patient's condition. Neither the insurance company nor "cover your ass" legal requirements should be the deciding factor in making any decision regarding diagnostic testing.

It also requires not unnecessarily duplicating tests. This has become less of a factor than in the past due to many of the tests being stored electronically and easier to share among physicians. While all the previously listed factors are important, they're actually symptoms that are covering up a very important truth.

The real key to reducing medical costs over the long term is to improve our health. While that seems obvious, many people fail to recognize all the factors in our current society that make improving our health increasingly difficult. These factors are all things that we collectively control, and every one of them stems from either greed in business or poor lifestyle choices.

Many of our current health problems come from chemical and genetic farming (which pollutes our air, water, ground, and bodies), chemicals from industrial waste, and too many sedentary lifestyle choices. Chemically-laden and genetically altered foods are poisoning our bodies. This only happens because *we keep buying poison-laden food.* **We are paying the food companies to poison us.** This choice is seriously harming our lives, and our lives in fact depend on changing this. Future generations are depending on us to change this. We'll get further into this later in this chapter, but for now it's important to know that any measures we take to control our health care costs will only be stop-gap measures unless we find a way to stop polluting our bodies and our world. If we don't find a way to stop this process, we will ultimately succeed in killing off the Earth and humanity.

We will need to in part reform our legal system.
Clearly many things about our legal system work as intended. However, there is too much latitude granted to those who choose to abuse the system. In addition, our legal system is used in some cases as a way to excessively punish those who have done wrong – even if that wrong was inadvertent, unavoidable, or due to circumstances truly beyond someone's control.

Although it may be difficult to establish clear and functional guidelines, we'll need to find a way to curtail both nuisance suits and excessive financial awards "to send a message." Both of these do not in any way support the true purpose of our legal system. In the case of nuisance suits, the courts need to establish a way to punish system abusers. Perhaps judges can, in clear and obvious cases, be given the latitude (which they may already have) to add court fines to court expenses in cases that clearly abuse the system. There are people who work within the system daily who have ideas about how this can be done. The key point is to recognize the problem first, then decide what steps to take to correct it. Then we can work out the details of those steps to accomplish our goal.

Another significant factor affecting our legal system, and one that ripples out to affect businesses and people, comes from some juries granting excessive awards as punishment for or as a message to businesses. These punitive damages affect later cases, so the damage wrought from this behavior escalates over time. While it's important to punish wrongdoers, awarding excessive punitive payments amounts to ultimately passing the buck to the business's customers. Therefore, excess awards issued as punishments tend to backfire by hurting customers and not the business directly. While this may do some public relations damage to the business, it's important to remember that business assets predominantly come from their customers. It makes no sense to punish a business for wrongdoing in a way that can be passed on as a cost to its customers. It's difficult to know what other options could work, and financial awards are currently the easiest way to inflict punishment on a business, but we'll need to work toward a better system for the future.

Social Security
This is obviously a big nut to crack, and has been for decades. Interestingly, Social Security will not be a long-term problem in a spiritual Republic for several reasons: 1) As the population grows more spiritual, greater numbers of people will embrace the idea of self-responsibility and fewer will depend on the government; 2) The government will grow smaller and less expensive to operate; and 3) The country as a whole will grow more prosperous. This will lead to more citizens becoming financially independent and businesses becoming more profitable – resulting in more tax revenue to meet the growing Social Security obligations. At some point down the road, it may become feasible to phase out Social Security entirely since fewer and fewer people will depend on it. This may seem radical and cold-hearted, but keep in mind that this country existed

for 159 years after the Declaration before Social Security was enacted.

Keeping Social Security solvent in the mid-term, however, will require some changes. Here are a few changes that should keep Social Security solvent long enough to reduce its outflow to more manageable levels:

- We need to reduce the costs of operating a business in the U.S.. This will reduce the number of jobs leaving our country for more favorable tax havens. The simplest way to do this is to gradually drop the corporate tax rate and the capital gains tax rate by 5 percent per year to a flat 15% each. While this may cause a temporary dip in business tax revenues, this dip will vanish as businesses stay in this country and become more profitable, thereby increasing taxes collected.

- Gradually raise the retirement eligibility age to 72. While many people will squawk at this, it's essential to realize that people have longer life spans now than they did at Social Security's inception, and this has had a major negative impact on a system that wasn't designed to handle payouts that can, at times, extend into several decades. Modest changes now will help both current and future generations.

- Set a target date to allow Americans to opt out of the Social Security system. That date will need to be announced at least 10 years before inception, and 15 would be better. Anyone that enters the work force after that target date will be able to opt out of the system and won't have deductions withheld. As a result, they won't receive any payouts at retirement. Allowing this time gives people enough time to prepare, but it also allows more time for more people to become spiritually aware and to embrace self-responsibility. People who have been in the system and paying Social Security up to that point will be able to opt out as well, but their benefits will need to be based on the point at which they opt out and capped at that calculated amount.

- As mentioned earlier, it's important to change retirement account regulations. Phase out deductions after revising the tax code to a simpler graduated flat tax. The next step is not limiting retirement deposits so families can choose on their own how much to save for their future. While it's true that some families may not be able to save much initially, bearing responsibility for their future may help them to make positive lifestyle changes that will increase their lifetime income. In addition, the previously mentioned decrease in the corporate tax rate should, over time, increase the pay rate for some jobs and increase job availability.

It's likely that we'll need to do more than this to reorganize the Social Security system, but everything needs a starting point. Taking steps in the right direction will give us more time and the opportunity to look a bit further down the road so we can see what corrective actions need to follow these initial suggested changes.

American businesses will need to overwhelmingly transition to honest and ethical business operations to reduce government regulation.
American businesses *can* operate ethically and still generate a profit. Although profits may initially decline in businesses that are maximizing profit at the expense of their customers and employees, in the long run those profits will be recovered by decreased government regulation and a decrease in costs associated with regulatory compliance. These companies will still have some costs from voluntarily meeting requirements, but we all know that reducing the size of bureaucracy has a positive affect on business bottom lines.

Many businesses already do operate honestly and ethically, and those businesses are currently being forced to pay regulatory costs they wouldn't have needed to pay if a small number of businesses hadn't tried to cheat the system. As is common in our government, the rule is to punish the majority that did nothing wrong to stop the few who try to get away with dishonest business dealings. This is clearly a short-sighted way to operate, and only businesses that won't self-regulate and that try to cheat the system should be held responsible for their actions. Unethical businesses will be punished for their actions individually, rather than regulating whole business segments and businesses that didn't do anything wrong. In this way we're encouraging businesses to make the right choice on their own.

157

Therefore, all business owners and managers who are currently cutting corners and cheating their employees or customers need to stop this activity. If your business can't survive without cheating others, then it's not viable on its own and you're stealing from them. Restructure your business to generate ethical profit or find a different business that can be run both ethically and profitably. If you don't want to do either, then close or sell your business. Honest and ethical business owners and managers won't want to deal with you anyway. This is the wave of the future, so join in or get out.

Encourage greater self-responsibility in American citizens.
Many Americans *do* take complete responsibility for their lives and well-being. However, many do not. Those who do not will need to learn to embrace a greater measure of self-responsibility. True freedom isn't possible without genuine self-responsibility. Keep in mind that self-responsibility doesn't mean you can't ask for help from others when you need it. Far from that. Helping each other is the reason we form communities in the first place. True self-responsibility starts with learning about all the different things that can cause problems for you and your family, and then preparing to meet those conditions in the best way you can. It's the opposite of an entitlement mentality, which is not believing it's necessary to be prepared since someone else – typically the government – will bail you out. It's probably obvious by now that entitlement thinking doesn't fit in well with a spiritual Republic.

Each of us taking greater responsibility for our lives, the lives of our families, and to a lesser degree for being able to help others in the community, is an essential step in forming a spiritual Republic. Since self-responsibility is a natural law, taking steps to take responsibility is a step toward a more spiritual perspective. This includes taking steps to be self-responsible in preserving your life and your family's lives against threats. This responsibility was well-recognized during the time of the Framers. Cesare Beccaria, an Italian author quoted by Thomas Jefferson, wrote the following passages in his collection of essays entitled *Of Crimes and Punishments*, published in 1764:

> "The laws of this nature are those which forbid to wear arms, disarming those only who are not disposed to commit the crime which the laws mean to prevent. Can it be supposed,

that those who have the courage to violate the most sacred laws of humanity, and the most important of the code, will respect the less considerable and arbitrary injunctions, the violation of which is so easy, and of so little comparative importance? Does not the execution of this law deprive the subject of that personal liberty, so dear to mankind and to the wise legislator? and does it not subject the innocent to all the disagreeable circumstances that should only fall on the guilty? It certainly makes the situation of the assaulted worse, and of the assailants better, and rather encourages than prevents murder, as it requires less courage to attack unarmed than armed persons."

From this passage it's plain to see that the right of self-protection, as a part of the principle of self-responsibility, has been regarded as a part of our liberty for at least some centuries, and perhaps even millennia. When citizens are able to protect their life with necessary force, the only disadvantage that arises is to the criminal. I'm sure many law-abiding citizens, if not all, support the idea of making crimes more difficult for criminals to commit. Not stripping the natural right of self-protection from citizens who wish to take responsibility for their well-being is a certain way to make it more difficult for criminals to commit crimes. There will be no debate about this in a spiritual Republic, and there should be none here in the United States either. People in this country are free to choose to be a victim, as are people who choose self-protection. For some to ask others to give up this right is a travesty that only benefits criminals. Much of this happens because people tend to focus specifically on guns, while the true problem is the *people* committing the crimes. Let's focus on that aspect of crime so we can do something meaningful about it without stripping away our natural right to self-protection – which, in fact, is not the government's to strip away. It's a right that is *recognized* by the Second Amendment; it's not *granted* by the Second Amendment. To sum it up, it's important to understand that all of society benefits when its *people* properly take personal responsibility for their lives.

So how do we get more people to take personal responsibility?

We need to start with the group that benefits the most from government programs. We need to shift the focus of their thinking from *entitlement* to *assistance*. This means changing the nature of our current public assistance programs. Various changes will be necessary, but the most important will be to place some value on the funds paid out by incorporating training programs and ultimately part-time work in preparation for full-time employment. This will work best when coupled with a business-friendly tax environment that leads to business growth, instead of the less than favorable environment we currently have. It will take some time and work, and there are many details that have to be hammered out, but helping people to become productive is a great way to build their self-esteem and sense of self-worth. Both are necessary in order to develop a sense of self-responsibility. Remember that this can be done, and we can start this process by electing local officials who understand the benefits that come from this approach, and by holding those officials accountable if they promise and don't deliver.

Make our food wholesome and nutritious again, as it has been in the past.
The frankenfoods we've created are clearly harming our collective health. More people are obese, more are diabetic, and incidences of serious conditions such as heart disease and cancer continue to increase as well. Anyone who puts any serious thought into this has to realize that these problems don't exist because we lack a particular drug or cure. They're happening because we're *causing* them by what we've done to our food and our environment. We can change this, and we need to do so *now*.

Only a few companies control our food supply right now, and yes, those few companies have significant resources. However, those resources *came from us*. They have a lot of capital because we buy their frankenfoods. If we stop buying, they'll no longer have huge revenues and huge resources. All it will take is for people to place their health and well-being, and their family's health and well-being, above convenience. I'd hope that every parent believes their children's well-being is a high priority. If that's true, then take some time to educate yourself about all the unhealthy ingredients that are in foods most children eat. Excessive amounts of sugar are extremely harmful, yet it's likely that most children regularly eat at least a *half pound* of sugar a day. Get a kitchen scale and pour out a half pound of sugar. Do you *really* want your children to eat that?

Do *you* want to eat that? Yet you are, and so are they. If you don't believe it, look at all the labels for the foods you feed your family. Find all the sugars and add them up. 28 grams equals 1 ounce, so add up the grams and divide by 28. You should include soft drinks, whether sodas, sport drinks, other sweetened drinks, or sweetened coffee or tea. If you do this, you'll see how much of a problem this really is.

Only you can fix this problem, and you fix it by not buying sugar-laden foods. You'll need to learn all the other names for sugar, such as sucrose, glucose, dextrose, maltodextrin, and one of the worst, high fructose corn syrup. It will mean preparing more foods from single ingredients, rather than out of a box. But isn't your child's health worth it? Isn't yours? If your answer isn't "yes," then you have some serious soul-searching to do. In case you're thinking the solution may be artificial sweeteners, you'll want to research what they are, and the real effects from consuming them, before you make that choice. Don't limit your research to government agencies since they have a vested interest in supporting business and not your health. Look deeper, and look into independent research. You may find Google Scholar helpful with this.

As large of a problem as it is, sugar isn't the only problem. Eating as much organic produce as you can afford will help, as will buying local foods as much as possible. Also consider avoiding GMO foods. These have various chemicals added into the plant's DNA *by viruses*. That's clearly not natural, and this practice assures that you're feeding your family dangerous chemicals (many of which are pesticides and herbicides. By the way, -cide means "to kill"). Avoiding feedlot meats in favor of small-farm meats will help as well. Educate yourself so you can make informed decisions that will help your family to be much healthier, now and into the future. Your family's health is at stake. What you feed your family now will affect their future in more ways than you realize. You can help them now, and help them later, by giving them fresh foods and by teaching them to eat fresh, healthful foods instead of the commercial convenience foods that are most likely leaving them lacking in micronutrients while harming their health.

Develop renewable, sustainable, and long-lasting sources of clean energy.

There is no longer any doubt that we need to develop energy sources free of fossil fuels. Even if you don't believe fossil fuels play any role in global warming, you surely must realize that they are a *finite* source of energy. Fossil fuels create considerable pollution, and that pollution hurts our bodies and the planet. At a minimum, it's irresponsible to add to the problems we're causing future generations because we haven't sought out and developed reasonable solutions. That's not at all a spiritual perspective, and it's not at all how citizens of a spiritual Republic think.

We have the technological capability to develop clean, renewable sources of energy. All it will take is some time, effort, and funding. This source of development would be an excellent use of government funds since the outcome ultimately benefits all Americans for generations. As Americans, we need to pressure our elected representatives to stop wasting money on things that don't make a real difference in our daily lives. We need to pressure them to use that money to help develop the energy sources we need now and into the future.

One significant point we need to keep in mind as we're doing this is that each form of energy we develop needs to be commercially viable. Each form of energy has to be independently profitable so companies can afford to operate and stay in business. This means no form of energy should be developed that would require government subsidies to remain viable. Subsidies should only be provided during research, development, and introduction. The reason for this is that energy subsidies are paid out of the profits of other businesses. In a spiritual Republic, the government would only choose to subsidize technologies that will fulfill a future need and will operate profitably. If a form of energy can't be produced profitably, it makes no sense to steal profits from other businesses in perpetuity just to support a business that will never support itself.

The major problem in replacing fossil fuels is in creating fuel for vehicles. Electric vehicles do serve an important purpose, but they can't currently replace trucks on the highway, or trains that do not currently have electrified tracks. If funding weren't an issue, it would be possible to create roadways that provide additional power to electric vehicles to extend their range. These roadways could incorporate embedded rails that provide current and are solar powered for at least some of the year, and would be most practical in sunny locations without annual snow. In time, and as technology advances, most of the current limitations on some of these technologies can be overcome. As with most new ideas, this could be tested on a small scale and then slowly spread into other areas a bit at a time. We could have a long-term functional system in place in about 4 to 5 decades. That may seem like a long time, but that time will pass fairly quickly and we can only reach our goal of clean energy by doing a little at a time over a long period of time. The most important thing we can do is to begin with what we think is best based on what we know right now. We can't finish what we never start.

We need to take more steps to pollute less and to clean our environment for our children and future generations.
Clean energy will help with less pollution, but it's not enough on its own to clean up the mess we already have. Many areas in this world are highly polluted due to industries that have no concern for the environment and want only to maximize profits. While this is currently the norm, businesses in a spiritual Republic will be far more conscientious about maintaining the environment and keeping it clean. So how do we get there from here?

Government pollution standards will help, but by themselves won't solve the problem. Unfortunately, the one change that is most important is to reduce greed in business owners and managers. Once we've largely overcome greed, getting responsible business owners and managers to take action will be much easier. They'll completely understand that they can help protect the world by trading a few of their profit dollars for a cleaner environment to leave to our heirs.

Helping the population to grow into greater spiritual awareness will help eliminate greed over the long run, and there is another, smaller interim step we can take to start the process sooner. Let's start teaching our children – from college right down to grade school – the importance of land stewardship. Start educating our youth to continue the work we've only just begun. It should be relatively simple to add this into school's curricula, and it's probably being taught in some areas already.

Another thing we can do is to harness the power of the devices so many people have become attached to – cell phones and tablets. There is probably a reasonable way to introduce a free app that will remind people daily of small things they can do to help our environment. Perhaps such an app exists already. Small things add up over time, and these small effects can add to big changes over the next 10 or 20 years. All we'd need is a visionary who is passionate about the environment, and who has the necessary tech savvy, to create and release one or more apps to spread the word and get others to take small actions.

Something else we can do is to look into putting GMO science to positive uses. My friend Renee shared an interesting idea with me. She suggested that we use GMO technology to create species of trees that metabolize a larger amount of CO_2 than trees do right now. It's probable that very little harm could come from that if these aren't trees that produce food, but having trees that have a greater capacity to reduce carbon dioxide would provide a substantial benefit with little or no harm. While this may not be a substantially profitable enterprise, it may be viable enough to get some government funding while the idea is tested and to launch it if it's viable. Other creative ideas surely exist, and each time we take action and improve a piece of our environment, no matter how insignificant it seems, we have made a positive step toward preserving our planet for our descendents.

Make natural methods of home building commercially viable.
A tremendous amount of good can be done by focusing on this step. Naturally built homes are better for the environment, better for the health of the occupants, and last much longer than the conventionally built homes of today. There are many reasons for this.

Naturally built homes have less impact on the environment from the moment they're being built right up until they're eventually demolished – which could easily be after several *centuries* of use. The materials are almost universally found locally, and have less impact on the environment since few natural homes use chemically processed materials. Most naturally-built homes, at the end of their useful life, can be returned to the ground or, in some cases, even composted.

164

Using natural materials means the occupants of the house will be exposed to fewer chemicals, and that can't ever be a bad thing for health. Naturally built houses often have solar and/or wind generated electric power (depending on what is appropriate for the area). Labor tends to be the most expensive part of the building process, but much of these labor-intensive processes can be mechanized to some degree for professional homebuilders. Due to the type of construction, which typically involves using a lot of mass (generally earth or stone), most properly designed naturally built homes have far lower utility costs to heat and cool them.

There are various options for building natural homes, and there are many resources that lay out the benefits of each type of construction. Here is a summary of some of the most popular options:

Rammed earth. This can be a difficult way for an individual to build a home since it requires highly compressing damp earth to create walls that are, on average, about 2 feet thick. This degree of compression requires machinery to compress the earth, but the resulting walls are massively stronger than walls built conventionally. They can withstand enormous changes in weather, and will survive when conventionally built homes are left in a pile of rubble. Properly built and maintained, this type of house could readily survive 300 years or more. When its useful life is over, the walls can be broken down and used as landfill – or even made into new walls.

Cob. This one is a mud monkey's dream. Using a properly proportioned mix of earth, clay, and straw, many homebuilders are able to, over time and with a bit of help, mix cob and build it into a (generally) small home. With natural plasters, a proper foundation, and a good roof with large overhangs, a cob home can also last for centuries. In fact, there are many cob homes in England and Scotland where there is a great deal of bad weather. In those locations, properly built cob homes have been measured to "wear" at the rate of an inch per *century*. Since cob walls are often 18-24 inches thick, you and many generations of families will be able to enjoy a properly built, comfortable cob home.

Adobe. This is similar to cob, except the earth mix is fashioned into bricks that are bound together to form walls. Many homes in the Middle East and the American Southwest are made of adobe and have stood for centuries as well.

Straw bale construction. Straw bales are stacked and interlocked to create walls, then covered with natural plasters to protect them from the elements. Straw bales provide a high degree of insulation and can be stacked fairly readily into walls by most people with some time, some help, and a willingness to do some hard work.

Timber frame with straw-clay filler. The first step is constructing a traditional timber frame (not a 2X4 stick frame – a frame built with heavy timbers). The sections between the timbers are then filled with straw that has been mixed with a thin clay mixture. This combines the strength of the timber frame with the insulating power of the straw.

There are other natural building techniques available, but these are a few of the major techniques currently in use. All of these methods of building are compatible with electrical systems, heating systems, and plumbing systems, so you won't need to be without modern comforts and conveniences to have a stronger and more healthful home. If you're interested in finding out more about natural houses, look for books by Daniel Chiras. He has a number of them that are well-written and clearly explain the various options.

Let's get back to "old-fashioned" family values.
I placed "old-fashioned" in quotes because many people reading this will think that some of these ideas are outmoded. However, the types of things I'll be covering in this section are actually "evergreen" rather than old-fashioned. In other words, these are ideas that our ancestors recognized as important, and they're just as important today – even though we've largely lost sight of them.

"Quantity" of life has surely replaced "quality" of life in many of today's families. Both parents and children are driven to the point of exhaustion trying to fit in as much as is humanly possible into their day. I believe this is a mistake on several levels. Often it's a drive to keep kids "busy" or occupied in some way. What's missing when we do this is teaching our kids how to be calm, quiet, reflective, and comfortable with their own thoughts. Trying to avoid this by keeping children fully occupied (including planting them in front of the TV for videos or games) teaches them that only *external* stimulation can keep their mind "busy." It does nothing to teach them how to think, and this often leads to "I'm bored."

Instead, try slowing down the pace of your life and your children's lives. Fit less into the day and stop driving your family to exhaustion. Teach your children that there are different ways to live, and that it's OK to live differently than your neighbors do. Show them how to be satisfied with what they have and how to appreciate their life as it is, instead of whining about what they don't have that all the other kids have. Naturally, parents will need to know how to do this before they can teach their children.

Let's teach our children that there is more to life than their phones, the internet, and TV. Get everyone away from their little screens and learn to interact again. We're creating a whole society of adolescents who believe a connection exists with someone else because they saw a post online. *This is not a connection. It is an illusion of connection.* Plan time together as a family. Include meals and conversation, regardless of how "boring" the kids may think it is at first. Turn off the TV's and all the little devices a few times a week and play some board games or cards. Teach them patience, and that we don't always win in life. But even so, we get up and keep going. Teach them that adversity can help them to do things better, and making mistakes helps to improve them as a person. Tell them why it's important to grow as a person. Teach them that it's OK for people to have different opinions than they do, and they can still get along with people even when they believe differently in some ways.

Let's bring back courtesy and politeness. Let's bring back respect, including self-respect. There is absolutely no down side to treating others with courtesy and respect. Many children these days do not have a real understanding of this, so we, as parents and grandparents, are responsible for teaching them how to be polite and why being polite is important. Let's also teach them how to resolve differences by reasoning and understanding. Show them how to see things from other's points of view so they can learn to resolve situations in ways that are agreeable to everyone involved.

All of this will require time and energy, so parents will need to slow down their frenetic pace too. Providing calm and reasonable guidance to your children is difficult if you're stressed and exhausted. Remember that children learn by example, so it's important to set the best example you can. It won't be easy, but few worthwhile things ever are. Think about the value this will have for your children and for future generations. This is what makes the extra effort worthwhile. It's easy to dismiss these ideas out of hand by deciding they're unimportant, but making that decision would be a mistake. If we look at this honestly, most people who dismiss these ideas will do so because they already feel overwhelmed. Instead of admitting this, which could seem like a weakness, some people would rather believe these ideas are unimportant or old-fashioned and don't fit in with today's society. That is completely wrong, and today's society seriously needs more courtesy, politeness, and respect among its citizens.

Restoring these three things, along with restoring family values, will significantly change our society for the better. Interactions will be less negative, and less negativity is good for society. People learning to think again, rather than being at the mercy of constant input from questionable sources, means all of us will become more accepting of different viewpoints since we'll be better able to see things from multiple perspectives. This could lead to fewer violent interactions since people in society will have a greater capacity for reason, greater acceptance, a better ability to understand others' perspectives, and a greater ability to defuse situations.

In addition to all these benefits, restoring family values and family interactions will strengthen your family's bond. You'll spend more time with your family instead of doing too many things apart from each other. If you do this, as your life approaches its end you'll be able to look back with satisfaction rather than regret. Regret is a painful negative emotion and a bad way to end your time on Earth. Make changes now to ensure that doesn't happen to you.

People need to learn more about spirituality and become more spiritual.
Spirituality is an essential part of building a spiritual Republic. More of our population needs to become aware of the true nature of spirituality, rather than holding on to the limited view we have of it

now from our current religious organizations. As I've mentioned before, there is a significant difference between religious organizations and spiritual principles, but these two are fairly entwined in this country. I firmly believe much of the resistance that some people have right now to spirituality is primarily a resistance to religious organizations.

I also believe that most people in this country would agree with many of the root principles I shared in the Spirituality section of this book. There is far more information to share about spirituality than I put into that section. Although it's a good place to start, it's even smaller than the proverbial "tip of the iceberg" in terms of how much we can learn about spirituality, and how much we can benefit from applying those principles to our daily lives. All you need to start with is a willingness to give it a try. Learn more about spiritual principles and begin applying them in your daily life. See for yourself that things work out better for everyone when you have a broader perspective and a greater understanding of how things interrelate. Find out for yourself what it's like to be calmer and have less stress. See how that influences your relationships with your family and others. There is absolutely nothing to lose by trying, other than the time you will have spent reading and studying spiritual principles.

Once you verify these principles and their benefits for yourself, others will begin to notice positive changes and may ask you about them. Share the truth with them when they ask. Tell them about what you've been learning that's helped you, and how it may be able to help them. Also begin to teach these principles to your children. Help them to become independent thinkers, and teach them how to apply spiritual principles in their lives. Teach them that life is better when they participate in it and interact directly with people instead of through phones and the internet. Let's get back to family values, add in the benefits of a truly spiritual perspective, and share this improvement with others. Once we do, we'll be well on our way to creating a spiritual Republic in the United States.

Part 7: What readers can do next

Never underestimate the power of making a choice and taking action. Nothing will change for the better if we don't take action to make changes for the better. As Gandhi said, "You must be the change you wish to see in the world." In that spirit, here are a few things that you can do, in case you need somewhere to start:

If you like the book, tell others about it. This is the most grass-roots way of spreading these ideas. If you agreed with at least parts of the premise, the ideas, and the ideals presented in this book, then your friends may benefit from reading it too. Tell them about *A Spiritual Republic* so they can read it and form their own opinion. This simple act can have many positive outcomes and it's very easy to do.

Get some people together who are reading or have read the book and discuss some of the ideas presented. If several of your friends are reading this book, then take the next step and talk about the concepts I've presented. Some of these ideas may appeal to some of your group, and group discussions can lead to even more and better ideas. The most important step is to take some form of action because nothing happens until we do.

Buy a few copies and give them as gifts or donate them to your local library. This goes a step further than telling your friends about it. This idea would work well with the idea of creating a discussion group with the friends you're gifting. Donating books to the library can help spread the word among people you may not know. The more people who read this book the faster we can make positive, lasting changes to our society.

Form a group to take action, brainstorm ideas and decide who can do what. This is a step past a book discussion group. In this group everyone is ready to take at least *some* action. This is a very powerful step since it's the first in a series of steps that can lead to real change. Not the false "hope and change" we were previously sold, but real, lasting improvements that can, one step at a time, transition America into the spiritual Republic that it can be. Achieving our goal of transitioning America into a spiritual Republic, while it may take decades, ensures that this country will

171

survive our current crises and endure for possibly hundreds or even thousands of years. It all starts with these 5 little letters: *a c t i o n.*

Write book review on Amazon.com. Writing an honest review on Amazon.com can help spread the word, especially if it's a favorable review. Honesty is essential, and I'm sure plenty of naysayers will chime in, but that makes it even more important for the supporters of these ideas to get onto Amazon and post their review as well.

Blog about *A Spiritual Republic* or write about it in forum posts. Millions of people read blogs and forums so this can be another powerful way to spread the word about the ideas in this book. This can lead to online book discussions and a greater likelihood of receiving search engine traffic on related key words.

Get more involved in your community. This country is a collection of communities. Every positive step taken at every level helps and improves the whole. Get to know your neighbors better, if you don't already. Find groups in your area that hold book discussions about spiritual topics. Join them and suggest *A Spiritual Republic.*

Make your views known at city council meetings. At first, attend some city council meetings to learn how they operate. Once you're familiar with the process, plan on sharing your views on topics important to you whenever discussion is open and appropriate.

Consider running for local office or State House Representative. We need to get more spiritually aware people into all levels of our government. That's the only way to deepen the spiritual perspective of our legislators, and it's a vital step toward achieving a spiritual Republic. After some local and State House experience, consider running for State Senate and, in time, perhaps the U.S. Senate or even a state Governorship. If some of us do this, the percentage of spiritually aware people in various levels of our government will grow over time, and it's probable that we will eventually have a President who is spiritually awake, or even a spiritual master. Such a person will be concerned with the highest good of all and will not be seduced by power and greed. That will truly be a turning-point event in our history and a powerful step in helping the United States become a real spiritual Republic.

Stop buying foods that are poisoning you and your family. The only reason large agribusinesses get away with selling us pseudo foods that are poor food choices is we keep buying them. Many people blindly trust Federal departments and reason that "they wouldn't sell it if it wasn't safe." These things are sold because that's where the profit is and the government is essentially in the pocket of big business. Money gets things approved, and biased "studies" say they're safe so poor products are waved through, even when most of the ingredients are artificial and, at best, don't really supply the nutrients your body needs to function properly. It will take a bit more time and effort, but you can fairly easily make fresh foods that are far better for your children than what comes out of a box, and you can also ensure they eat less sugar and fewer chemicals as a result. You may find that fresh foods help your children to be healthier and possibly even better behaved. In addition to fresher foods with less sugar, get your children accustomed to filtered or distilled water instead of sugary drinks and sodas. Their bodies don't need the sugar or, even worse, any artificial sweeteners and artificial colors you'll find in most soft drinks. Fewer chemical coloring agents will be better for your children than what they are probably consuming now.

By reducing your family's consumption of sugar, corn and genetically-altered frankenwheat, their health will improve and you'll also be helping the planet by supporting non-chemical agriculture. Doing this begins to weaken the largest food producers by decreasing their revenues. In time they'll notice the drop in revenues, and they'll eventually need to deliver the healthful food people want or go out of business. If you stay away from GMO (genetically modified organism) food products, buy organic when possible, shop farmers markets when possible and find local sources of clean meats, you'll be providing the best food you can for your family and helping the rest of us (and the planet) in the process.

Be a family again. iPods, iPads, phones, and similar digital devices have overtake our society. Some people are as dependent on them as they would be on some drugs. This is both unhealthy and unwise. It's a bad example to set for our children, and it's bad for us as adults too. From a spiritual perspective, living your life won't happen through a viewscreen. You have to be an active participant and actually do things, rather than live virtually. Let's collectively

173

decrease our dependence on iPods, iPads, our phones, and the Internet. Let's teach children how to think, instead of teaching them to require constant input and media bombardment. Help them to be comfortable with their own thoughts, and help them understand that it's OK to not have every little device that everyone else seems to have and be addicted to. Teach them to value their family. Teach them about respect and self-respect. Teach them spiritual principles. Instill spiritual values that will help guide many future generations.

Spiritual steps

Here are a few things you can do to learn more about spirituality and to incorporate it into your everyday life:

Read spiritually-based books. There are many to choose from, but there are a few that strike very close to the mark and have very accurate and very specific spiritual information. The books that I find closest to my understanding of deep spiritual principles are a series by Ronna Herman (who now uses the surname Vezane, but her books are still under her former name). This series of books contains spiritual messages from Archangel Michael channeled by Ronna. I first learned of these books in late 2013, so most of my spiritual growth didn't come from these books directly. However, when I read them, I recognized that I was reading spiritual information that I already knew to be true. That's the reason I'm recommending them.

In my opinion, it's helpful to already have some spiritual background to get the most out of the messages, but some of that background isn't included in the books. My previous book, *A Different View of the World,* helps to bridge that gap. I'm also working on a spiritual study guide for my students that will provide more background information and define the unfamiliar terms used throughout this book series. I've only just begun to work on it, but this guide should be ready by late 2015. If you're reading this book at or after that time, check for the guide on Amazon.com by searching my name. You may also find the guide in other book stores. Here are the book titles by Ronna Herman:

On Wings of Light
The Golden Promise
Your Sacred Quest

Let There Be Light
Revealed Cosmic Truths

Her website is www.ronnastar.com, and she has additional books and materials there as well.

Tell others about your new spiritual perspectives. As you learn spiritual ideas, it's helpful to tell others who may be interested about those ideas. Explaining the concepts improves your understanding and helps to spread these spiritual ideas and perspectives. If you're inclined to, you can tell them about Ronna's books and other resources you may know of. If you have several people interested it might be feasible to form book discussion groups, although it's best if those groups are led by someone with more experience and a deeper understanding of the content. If you don't have access to someone with a deeper understanding, have the discussions anyway since sharing ideas will help everyone grow.

Learn from me directly. First and foremost I am a spiritual teacher. Some people will be nearby and able to learn from me in person. However, with enough interest we can start building an online community, and that may spread into forming groups in local communities as well. That's something we can work on and develop if there is enough interest.

Learn from other spiritual teachers. There are many spiritual teachers in this world, and one of them may be just right for you. Search online and learn more about various teachers until you find one whose ideas appeal to you or with whom you feel some "resonance."

If none of these ideas appeal to you then take action in any way that does. Regardless of what it is or how small, take at least a tiny step each day and encourage others to take small steps too. Each step counts and brings us closer to realizing our goal of transforming America into a spiritual Republic.

Part 8: Conclusion

We can't stay on the downhill slope this country is currently careening down. That slope ends in ruin.

Future generations of Americans are counting on us to fix this mess and make it right. The quality of their lives and the level of freedom they will have depends a great deal on what you and I do today and every day.

If you had a knot in your gut at any point while reading this book, that knot is there because part of you recognizes the problems and wants to take action – so choose a place to start and take action today. Small actions add together, so please don't fall into the trap of thinking that the job is too big and small actions won't make any difference. *Every action counts,* and every day we wait makes our job a little bit harder. Let's be the people our forefathers wanted us to be. Let's restore the United States to the Republic it was meant to be. Then we can move forward to a form of government that could transform the world and last for thousands of years: the spiritual Republic.

Many people in our country have numerous excellent ideas for solving our nation's problems. It's time to marshal all our best resources and restore the United States' place in this world. Not as one nation plundered by many, but as a shining beacon showing the world what is truly possible when we embrace the spiritual birthright of humanity.

The solutions to these problems lie with the American people, and not with our government. We have to focus our efforts and set a goal to regain control of our government and wrest it out of the hands of the politicians who have done massive damage to our nation. Our government was supposed to be *by the people and for the people,* so let's return to those roots and take America to the real heights we can reach. It's not possible to reach those heights by settling for mediocrity. We have to do more. We have to *be* more. Each of us has to realize we all have a personal stake in what happens next in our country. We can roll over and let the politicians continue to bankrupt our country into utter ruin. Or we can stand up and say, "Enough!"

Either choice is ours to make, and our future is riding on this choice. Let's not shy away from hard work. Let's not take the easy way out. Let's secure our country's future in the only way that we can – as real and true AMERICANS. Let's restore liberty and cry out to the rest of the world, "Let FREEDOM Ring!" The road won't be easy, but it is vital that we take action. Many of us will need to learn more about the spiritual principles I've shared in this book and to realize that what I've shared can really happen. The United States can indeed become the world's first spiritual Republic. It's up to us, and it's up to us to start today.

Please raise up your voice and join me. Our future depends on it.

Kevin T. Adam
January, 2015

www.ingramcontent.com/pod-product-compliance
Lightning Source LLC
Chambersburg PA
CBHW071353280526
45787CB00001B/300